CONTENTS

WAYS IN TO THE TEXT

Who Is Was John C. Calhoun? 9

What Does *A Disquisition on Government* Say? 10

Why Does *A Disquisition on Government* Matter? 12

SECTION 1: INFLUENCES

Module 1: The Author and the Historical Context 15

Module 2: Academic Context 19

Module 3: The Problem 23

Module 4: The Author's Contribution 27

SECTION 2: IDEAS

Module 5: Main Ideas 32

Module 6: Secondary Ideas 36

Module 7: Achievement 40

Module 8: Place in the Author's Work 44

SECTION 3: IMPACT

Module 9: The First Responses 48

Module 10: The Evolving Debate 53

Module 11: Impact and Influence Today 58

Module 12: Where Next? 62

Glossary of Terms 67

People Mentioned in the Text 79

Works Cited 86

THE MACAT LIBRARY

The Macat Library is a series of unique academic explorations of seminal works in the humanities and social sciences – books and papers that have had a significant and widely recognised impact on their disciplines. It has been created to serve as much more than just a summary of what lies between the covers of a great book. It illuminates and explores the influences on, ideas of, and impact of that book. Our goal is to offer a learning resource that encourages critical thinking and fosters a better, deeper understanding of important ideas.

Each publication is divided into three Sections: Influences, Ideas, and Impact. Each Section has four Modules. These explore every important facet of the work, and the responses to it.

This Section-Module structure makes a Macat Library book easy to use, but it has another important feature. Because each Macat book is written to the same format, it is possible (and encouraged!) to cross-reference multiple Macat books along the same lines of inquiry or research. This allows the reader to open up interesting interdisciplinary pathways.

To further aid your reading, lists of glossary terms and people mentioned are included at the end of this book (these are indicated by an asterisk [*] throughout) – as well as a list of works cited.

Macat has worked with the University of Cambridge to identify the elements of critical thinking and understand the ways in which six different skills combine to enable effective thinking.
Three allow us to fully understand a problem; three more give us the tools to solve it. Together, these six skills make up the **PACIER** model of critical thinking. They are:

ANALYSIS – understanding how an argument is built
EVALUATION – exploring the strengths and weaknesses of an argument
INTERPRETATION – understanding issues of meaning

CREATIVE THINKING – coming up with new ideas and fresh connections
PROBLEM-SOLVING – producing strong solutions
REASONING – creating strong arguments

To find out more, visit **WWW.MACAT.COM.**

An Analysis of

John C. Calhoun's

A Disquisition on Government

Etienne Stockland
and
Jason Xidias

www.macat.com
info@macat.com

Cover illustration: Capucine Deslouis

Cataloguing in Publication Data
A catalogue record for this book is available from the British Library.
Library of Congress Cataloguing-in-Publication Data is available upon request.

ISBN 978-1-912303-19-9 (hardback)
ISBN 978-1-912128-73-0 (paperback)
ISBN 978-1-912282-07-4 (e-book)

Notice
The information in this book is designed to orientate readers of the work under analysis,
to elucidate and contextualise its key ideas and themes, and to aid in the development
of critical thinking skills. It is not meant to be used, nor should it be used, as a
substitute for original thinking or in place of original writing or research. References and
notes are provided for informational purposes and their presence does not constitute
endorsement of the information or opinions therein. This book is presented solely for
educational purposes. It is sold on the understanding that the publisher is not engaged
to provide any scholarly advice. The publisher has made every effort to ensure that
this book is accurate and up-to-date, but makes no warranties or representations with
regard to the completeness or reliability of the information it contains. The information
and the opinions provided herein are not guaranteed or warranted to produce particular
results and may not be suitable for students of every ability. The publisher shall not be
liable for any loss, damage or disruption arising from any errors or omissions, or from
the use of this book, including, but not limited to, special, incidental, consequential or
other damages caused, or alleged to have been caused, directly or indirectly, by the
information contained within.

CRITICAL THINKING AND *A DISQUISITION ON GOVERNMENT*

Primary critical thinking skill: PROBLEM-SOLVING
Secondary critical thinking skill: ANALYSIS

Nineteenth-century American politician John C. Calhoun occupies a paradoxical place in the history of political thought – and of critical thinking. On one hand, he is remembered as a committed advocate of slavery, consistently espousing views that are now considered indefensible and abhorrent. On the other, the political theories that Calhoun used to defend the social injustice of slavery have become the basis of the very systems by which modern democracies defend minority rights. Despite being crafted in defence of a system as unjust as slavery, the arguments that Calhoun expressed about minority rights in democracies in A Disquisition On Government remain an excellent example of how problem solving skills and reasoning can come together. The problem, for Calhoun, was both specific and general. As matters stood in the late 1840s, the majority of American states were anti-slavery, with only the minority, Southern states remaining pro-slavery. This boiled down to a crucial issue with democracy: the US government should not, Calhoun argued, only respect the wishes of the majority. Instead, democratic government must aim to harmonize diverse groups and their interests – governing, in so far as possible, for everyone. His analysis of how the Southern states could protect what he saw as their right to keep slaves led Calhoun to formulate solutions to the problem of 'the tyranny of the majority' that have since helped defend far worthier minority views.

ABOUT THE AUTHOR OF THE ORIGINAL WORK

Born in South Carolina in the United States in 1782, **John C. Calhoun** came from a family of prosperous farmers and slaveholders. An 1804 graduate of Yale University, he went on to have a distinguished political career that included US government posts as a South Carolina senator, secretary of war, secretary of state, and vice president. Concerned about overbearing government, Calhoun campaigned for the rights of individual states and remained a staunch supporter of slavery, views that were at the heart of tensions within the American Union. He died in 1850, 11 years before the start of the American Civil War.

ABOUT THE AUTHORS OF THE ANALYSIS

Etienne Stockland is researching a PhD in environmental history at Columbia University.

Dr Jason Xidias holds a PhD in European Politics from King's College London, where he completed a comparative dissertation on immigration and citizenship in Britain and France. He was also a Visiting Fellow in European Politics at the University of California, Berkeley. Currently, he is Lecturer in Political Science at New York University.

ABOUT MACAT

GREAT WORKS FOR CRITICAL THINKING

Macat is focused on making the ideas of the world's great thinkers accessible and comprehensible to everybody, everywhere, in ways that promote the development of enhanced critical thinking skills.

It works with leading academics from the world's top universities to produce new analyses that focus on the ideas and the impact of the most influential works ever written across a wide variety of academic disciplines. Each of the works that sit at the heart of its growing library is an enduring example of great thinking. But by setting them in context – and looking at the influences that shaped their authors, as well as the responses they provoked – Macat encourages readers to look at these classics and game-changers with fresh eyes. Readers learn to think, engage and challenge their ideas, rather than simply accepting them.

'Macat offers an amazing first-of-its-kind tool for interdisciplinary learning and research. Its focus on works that transformed their disciplines and its rigorous approach, drawing on the world's leading experts and educational institutions, opens up a world-class education to anyone.'

Andreas Schleicher
Director for Education and Skills, Organisation for Economic Co-operation and Development

'Macat is taking on some of the major challenges in university education … They have drawn together a strong team of active academics who are producing teaching materials that are novel in the breadth of their approach.'

Prof Lord Broers,
former Vice-Chancellor of the University of Cambridge

'The Macat vision is exceptionally exciting. It focuses upon new modes of learning which analyse and explain seminal texts which have profoundly influenced world thinking and so social and economic development. It promotes the kind of critical thinking which is essential for any society and economy. This is the learning of the future.'

Rt Hon Charles Clarke, former UK Secretary of State for Education

'The Macat analyses provide immediate access to the critical conversation surrounding the books that have shaped their respective discipline, which will make them an invaluable resource to all of those, students and teachers, working in the field.'

Professor William Tronzo, University of California at San Diego

WAYS IN TO THE TEXT

KEY POINTS

- John C. Calhoun was a firm defender of states' rights* and the practice of slavery.

- A *Disquisition on Government* argues that states should have the power to nullify* (invalidate) any law that they deem unconstitutional. The main reason Calhoun introduced this principle was to safeguard the practice of slavery in the American South.

- The text is a seminal work in American political philosophy: it has served as an important reference point for the defense of minority rights* against majority rule.*

Who Was John C. Calhoun?

John C. Calhoun was born in South Carolina in 1782. He earned a Bachelor of Arts degree at Yale College and then completed legal training at Tapping Reeve Law School in Connecticut. Afterwards, he served in the US Senate for 15 years and as secretary of war* (1817–25), vice president (1825–32), and then secretary of state (1844–45).

As a politician, Calhoun is most remembered for his strident defense of both states' rights—that is, the rights of individual states rather than the federal government—and the practice of slavery. His father, a plantation and slave owner, taught him that a partial reflection of a man's success was the number of slaves that he owned.[1] This upbringing shaped Calhoun's worldview as an adult. He also advocated for limited government and free trade, especially after his home state labored under federal tariffs* passed by US Congress* in the 1820s. During this time, Calhoun began to formulate the ideas at the core of *A Disquisition on Government.*

Calhoun believed that individual states should have the right to nullify any law that they deemed unconstitutional. Nullification* was a state's right to strike down any law that affected it, but that worked against its interests. This was an early defense of minority rights, a concept that remains important today.

Although Calhoun passed away in 1850, 11 years before the start of the American Civil War,* his staunch backing of states' rights and slavery actually inspired seven states in the American South to secede (break away) from the Union in 1861. They temporarily made up the Confederate States of America.*

In 1957, the United States Senate honored Calhoun as one of the five most important senators in American history. Future president John F. Kennedy* commended him for being a "forceful logician of state sovereignty" and a "masterful defender of the rights of a political minority against the dangers of an unchecked majority."[2]

What Does *A Disquisition on Government* Say?

Calhoun wrote *A Disquisition on Government* between 1843 and 1848 as an attempt to find an ideal form of government. Published in 1851 after his death, this work of American political philosophy argues that government's central aim should be to harmonize diverse groups—and their interests—within a society. Calhoun sees this as an important yet difficult task, as he believes that all individuals are inclined to choose self interest over the "common good." And because politics is practiced by individuals, government reflects self interest as well.

Calhoun concludes that, as a result of this, governments naturally tend towards oppression and tyranny unless checked by a constitution*—a set of political principles used to establish the state—that protects the particular interests of minority groups. Without such a check, a community or nation is doomed to plunge into anarchy and violence. Further, Calhoun argues, to keep dominant parties from abusing and consolidating power, a constitution had to be based on what he calls the "concurrent majority."* By concurrent majority, he means that minority groups should share influence with the "numerical majority"*—the group that the majority of voters elects—to keep it from wielding excessive power.

To put this power-sharing model into practice in America, Calhoun proposes that individual states should have the right to invalidate any law within their territorial boundaries that they consider against their interests. This tactic is known as nullification.* What's more, he proposes that any new law should require unanimous agreement among the states and the federal government. While he acknowledges a potential for gridlock in the political process, Calhoun argues that this "compromise" is necessary to safeguard the Union from breaking up. And to prove that it would work, he cites examples of the concurrent majority in action. He writes, for instance, about how a legislative body in which all members could veto* legal proceedings ruled the Kingdom of Poland.*

In spite of Calhoun's aims, his concurrent majority model never gained a foothold in American law. Article 4, Clause 2 of the American Constitution* stipulates that the federal government is the "supreme law of the land."

Aside from his broader goal of political reform, Calhoun also wrote *Disquisition* with the intent to protect slavery. Although he never directly states his pro-slavery stance in the text, his concept of nullification (along with the right to veto) applies to any central government law that frees slaves and jeopardizes the southern states'* economy.

Further, Calhoun supported the idea of a social order where a more intelligent and virtuous class of people ruled over those he saw as ignorant and degraded. He believed that civil rights and liberty should be denied to inferior peoples, and he thus provided a moral justification for slavery. By the dawn of the twentieth century, the views Calhoun expressed in *Disquisition* were dismissed as racist and favoring the rights of a privileged slave-owning minority.

So on the one hand, Calhoun penned *A Disquisition on Government* for statesmen and general readers who wanted to preserve the union between the North and South. But, on the other, he also sought to appeal to those who sympathized with the South's desire for political and economic freedom.

Why Does *A Disquisition on Government* Matter?

A Disquisition on Government defends minority rights and interests against the "tyranny" of a majority government.* Calhoun intended the text to have a direct bearing on conflicts between the North and South that threatened to tear the Union apart in the 1840s and 1850s. In the late 1840s, the United States added vast new territories following the Mexican–American War.* This action provoked sharp debates between pro-slavery and anti-slavery activists: would these new states join the Union as "free" states without slavery or as slave states?

Starting at roughly the same time in 1848, the Free Soil Party* (a group of anti-slavery activists) claimed that the US Congress had constitutional powers to abolish slavery in the southern states. However, this stance created strong tensions between the North and South. *A Disquisition on Government* avoids any specific mention of slavery or regional conflicts of the day. But its primary intent is to defend the practice of slavery, as southern politicians widely perceived the US government as dominated by northern abolitionists* who wanted to abolish it.

In the end, the abolitionists prevailed. After the American Civil War, the Thirteenth Amendment* to the American Constitution abolished slavery, and Calhoun's text fell largely out of favor. Well into the middle of the twentieth century, historians and political theorists accused Calhoun of being a racist who favored the rights of privileged minorities as opposed to minorities in general.

But this view of Calhoun and the *Disquisition* changed following the Holocaust* in World War II,* when the Nazi Party* majority in Germany exterminated more than six million Jews. Nazi actions under Adolf Hitler* illustrated the very "tyranny of the majority" that Calhoun had warned of in the nineteenth century. From the mid-twentieth century onward, various liberal thinkers and social activists have cited *A Disquisition on Government* as an argument for upholding minority rights. In particular, the Civil Rights Movement* and the formation of the United Nations* are cited as prime examples of Calhoun's theories in action. Calhoun's concept of a concurrent majority—where political action requires the unanimous consent of states—moved onto the world stage at the UN's Security Council, where any single member nation can stop action on a proposed measure.

In the twenty-first century, Calhoun's *Disquisition* will likely continue to influence debates on how to achieve balance between majority and minority interests in nations across the world.

NOTES

1   Irving H. Bartlett, *John Calhoun: A Biography* (New York and London: W.W. Norton & Company, 1993), 218.

2   "John C. Calhoun: A Featured Biography," *United States Senate* website, accessed February 25, 2015, https://www.senate.gov/artandhistory/ history/ common/generic/Featured_Bio_Calhoun.htm.

SECTION 1
INFLUENCES

MODULE 1
THE AUTHOR AND THE
HISTORICAL CONTEXT

KEY POINTS

- *A Disquisition on Government* tried to prevent the break-up of the United States, while defending the rights of slave owners and protecting the economic interests of the southern states.

- The text capped Calhoun's long political career as a South Carolina US senator, secretary of war,* secretary of state, and vice president.

- The rise of the anti-slavery movement and the increasing political influence of abolitionists* from the 1820s onwards provoked repeated threats of secession*— withdrawal from the United States—from pro-slave states. These developments shaped Calhoun's central argument in the text.

Why Read This Text?

A Disquisition on Government is one of the most important anti-federalist* writings of the nineteenth century. Anti-Federalists opposed a strong federal (centralized) government because they feared it would infringe on states' rights. Two prominent examples were Patrick Henry,* an attorney and politician from Virginia, and George Mason,* a politician and delegate from Virginia to the United States Constitutional Convention.*

The text displays the fear held by statesmen in Calhoun's time—along with political thinkers and plantation owners in the American South—of an increasingly powerful central government dominated by "northern interests." Above all, they feared that northern

> ❝ It is commonplace that John C. Calhoun is among America's greatest and most controversial statesmen ... He was also a political theorist of the first rank and was remarked as such when the term itself was still hardly known. ❞
>
> Guy Story Brown,* *Calhoun's Philosophy of Politics*

abolitionists would seize control of the federal government and abolish slavery. A growing "Nullification Party"* in the American South advocated the rights of states to strike down a law enacted by the US Congress.* This, in turn, raised the fear of armed conflict between the southern states* and the federal government. Calhoun's *Disquisition* attempts to avert such a conflict in three ways:

- Proposing a constitutional model to protect the institution of slavery.
- Preventing tyranny by federal politicians representing a "numerical majority"—whereby a state is dominated by a group elected through majority votes.
- Creating a compromise that would preserve the political unity of the United States.

Author's Life

John C. Calhoun (1782–1850) was born in the southwestern frontier of South Carolina to a family of prosperous Scotch-Irish* farmers and slaveholders. As a child, Calhoun attended a private academy run by a Presbyterian* minister in Appling, Georgia. There he received a classical education, studying Latin, ancient Greek, philosophy, and history. At the age of 17, his father became ill, requiring Calhoun to spend a short time working on his family's plantation.

Thanks to financial help from his brother, however, Calhoun was able to resume his studies. In 1804, he graduated from Yale College and returned to South Carolina to study law in Charleston under the prominent lawyer Henry William de Saussure.* Calhoun then completed his legal training in 1806 at a private academy in Litchfield, Connecticut. The sum of these experiences gave him a deep understanding of life in both the North and South.

Calhoun finished *Disquisition* in 1848, toward the end of his life, although the text was published posthumously in 1851. It capped a long political career that saw Calhoun assume the offices of South Carolina senator, secretary of war, secretary of state, and vice president. Calhoun's political career spanned a period of heightened political tension between pro-slavery interests in the American South and the federal government.

Author's Background

Debates regarding the relationship between the states and the federal government, as well as the prospect of a "tyranny of the majority"*—a fear that America's democracy* could turn into an oppressive political system—date back to the eighteenth century. Back then, the thirteen American colonies* had declared their independence from an abusive British monarchy,* which taxed colonists heavily while depriving them of representation in Britain's Parliament of Westminster.

In the 1790s, the Federalist* and Republican* parties formed in America. Federalists advocated a strong central government and defended the views of industry, while Republicans backed strong state rights* and represented the voices of farmers and plantation owners. The two parties then wrestled for control of the presidency, Congress, and state governments. The War of 1812* between America and Britain aggravated this competition. Republicans believed war was necessary because Britain had imposed restrictions on United States trade with France. But New England Federalist states, led by Massachusetts, opposed the war and refused to contribute their armies. They feared

17

that war would hurt their trade with both Britain and France.

From the 1820s onwards, the abolitionist movement in the northern states gained in organization and strength. This provoked repeated threats from pro-slavery southern states to secede from the United States. Calhoun's career was defined by his attempt to prevent this dissolution while protecting slave owners and economic interests in the southern states. At the heart of his defense was cotton, a highly profitable crop whose production depended heavily on slave labor. Within this tense political context, Calhoun introduced his two seminal concepts: 1) a "concurrent majority,"* whereby minority groups shared influence with the majority, and 2) a minority veto,* whereby states could overturn laws that threatened their interests.

MODULE 2
ACADEMIC CONTEXT

KEY POINTS

- When *A Disquisition on Government* was published, three major concerns dominated nineteenth century America: 1) the division of power among the federal* and state governments, 2) whether slavery should exist, and 3) the future political unity of the United States.

- Classical republicanism*— an ideology built on the concepts of mixed government, civic virtue and liberty— provided the backdrop for Calhoun's central argument in the text.

- The author drew from classical republican thought to argue that human nature was prone to conflict and oppression. He saw the best solution as a "concurrent majority,"* which would protect states' interests against a "tyranny of the majority."*

The Work in its Context

Throughout his political career, John C. Calhoun presented himself as a protector of the ideals promoted by the Founding Fathers* of the United States. These Founding Fathers were a group of statesmen and political leaders who participated in the American Revolution* and established the American Constitution.* *A Disquisition on Government* reflects the ideals of classical republicanism—those of morality, civic virtue, and the pursuit of the common good over self-interest—upon which the first statesmen in America were educated.

At the heart of the text is Calhoun's belief that human nature is imperfect. He argues that all individuals are prone to choose self

> **❝** Unlike other theorists who preceded or who would follow Calhoun, both American and European, he did not seek to invent a new mode of philosophical speculation or a 'grand theory' for the human sciences. Instead, he offered a refinement of classical, medieval, and modern notions regarding the relationship between government and social order. **❞**
>
> H. Lee Cheek Jr., *John C. Calhoun: Selected Writings and Speeches*

interest over the "common good." And because individuals instigate politics, government reflects self interest, as well. Both Aristotle* and the seventeenth-century English philosopher Thomas Hobbes,*among others, had previously expressed this view.

Calhoun saw politics both positively and negatively. On the one hand, some individuals could exercise their moral and intellectual beliefs for the good of society. On the other, those prone to vice were also part of the political process. Thus, government was a necessary evil to mediate between the two groups and head off sharp conflicts.

In *Disquisition*, Calhoun attempts to find an ideal form of government to balance individual liberties with the need for mediation. His core argument is that popular democracies* will deteriorate into a "tyranny of the majority"—a situation where the interests of the many overrule those of the few. His solution to this problem is a concurrent majority, or constitutional arrangement whereby a state could block any legislation that it deemed an action against the political and economic interests within its borders.

Overview of the Field

Calhoun's republicanism, however, was also marked by a conservatism typical of pro-slavery statesmen in the American South. In *Disquisition*, Calhoun rejects the theories of natural rights* and universal equality,* both of which back the inalienable rights of all humans. More-radical republicans, such as Thomas Paine,* promoted these concepts during the American Revolution* and French Revolution.* Yet in *Disquisition*, Calhoun writes that it was a "dangerous error to suppose that all people are equally entitled to liberty."

For Calhoun, liberty is a "reward to be earned, not a blessing to be gratuitously lavished on all alike." Thus, it should be reserved only for "the intelligent, the patriotic, the virtuous and deserving." He argues that civil rights* and liberty should be denied to people "too ignorant, degraded and vicious, to be capable either of appreciating or of enjoying it." This boils down to a racist ideology that justified the enslavement of black people, and provided a moral justification for the institution of slavery in the American South.[1]

Calhoun's most original contribution to republican political thought is the concept of a "concurrent majority." Popular democracy, Calhoun believed, would inevitably deteriorate into tyranny unless the constitution contained a mechanism that allowed minority states in a majority system to influence the political process. An example was the Tariff of 1828,* which Congress* passed to protect northern industry against foreign competition. As a result, Britain cut down exports to the United States, which in turn reduced the amount of cotton they bought from the American South. Calhoun viewed this as an unfair infringement on states' rights.

This concept, however, reflected and built on the writings of republican thinkers such as Thomas Jefferson* and James Madison.* During the drafting of the American Constitution,* they advocated limiting central government power while increasing the political influence of individual states. So the concept of a concurrent majority fell within an existing tradition of republican thought that favored decentralized government and a loose federation of individual states.

Academic Influences

Three of the most prominent Federalists* of the early republican period* that dated to the late eighteenth century were Calhoun's teachers. Federalists of this period supported the proposed American Constitution between 1787 and 1789, and advocated a republic built on a strong central government and limited sovereignty for American states. While enrolled at Yale College, Calhoun studied under the theologian and leading Federalist Timothy Dwight.* He then received his legal education in Charleston, South Carolina, and Litchfield, Connecticut, from two influential Federalist Party* members: Henry William de Saussure* and Tapping Reeve.*

Yet despite the leanings of his mentors, Calhoun became an outspoken critic of Federalist ideology and a strong defender of states' rights early on in his career. He felt that the federal government was oppressive because some of its policies benefited industry in the American North but hurt agriculture in the American South. The writings of Thomas Jefferson* and James Madison*—who, while drafting the American Constitution, had sought to check the power of central government and advocated for greater powers to individual states—influenced Calhoun's theory of the "concurrent majority." *Disquisition* bears the imprint of Jeffersonian republicanism.* This stream of thought, as updated by Calhoun, expresses the fear that popular governments, representing a "numerical majority,"* will abuse their power unless checked by a constitution that guarantees the equal political influence of minority groups and interests.

NOTES

1   *John C. Calhoun, A Disquisition on Government*, ed. H. Lee Cheek Jr. (South Bend, IN: St Augustine's Press, 2007), 41.

MODULE 3
THE PROBLEM

KEY POINTS

- Calhoun advocated the protection of states' rights against a "tyranny of the majority"* that sought to dominate them.
- A Disquisition on Government responded to the growing abolitionist* movement. Calhoun sought to safeguard the practice of slavery, which the southern economy depended heavily upon.
- The notion of a "tyranny of the majority" dates back to ancient Greece. John Adams,* the second president of the United States, was first to use the term, in 1788.

Core Question

John C. Calhoun's *A Disquisition on Government* asks a question that had long been central to political philosophy: "How can those who are invested with the powers of government be prevented from employing them as the means of aggrandizing themselves, instead of using them to protect and preserve societies?"[1] In other words, *Disquisition* seeks to outline a way to prevent popularly elected governments from becoming tyrannical, despotic* regimes.

To this end, Calhoun cites a "tyranny of the majority," where democracies* would dominate minority interests and states unless checked by a constitution* that balanced power among varying social groups within a state. Calhoun argues that it is essential to protect state interests against the prospect of this threat.

The concept of oppressive rule dates back to ancient Greece. But John Adams* appears to be the first to use the specific term "tyranny of the majority," in 1788.[2] Adams was the second president of the United States, a key figure of the American Revolution,* and a drafter

> ❝ The Union, next to our liberty, most dear! May we all remember that it can only be preserved by respecting the rights of the States, and distributing equally the benefits and burdens of the Union. ❞
>
> John C. Calhoun, Jefferson's Birthday Toast, cited in *The Essential Calhoun*

of the Declaration of Independence.* In reality, the phrase bears a striking resemblance to what James Madison* warned against in *Federalist Paper 10* in 1787: "the superior force of an interested and overbearing majority."[3] French political thinker and historian Alexis de Tocqueville* further popularized the phrase in his seminal work *Democracy in America* in 1835, and since then, many other scholars have used it, including British philosopher and political economist John Stuart Mill.*

The Participants

Aristotle* argued that a "mixed government"—one that combined democracy, an aristocracy of nobles, and a monarchy*—was ideal to balance the excesses he saw in pure democracies. Thinkers in the Italian Renaissance* such as Florentine historian and political philosopher Niccolò Machiavelli,* as well as the English Commonwealth men* in the seventeenth century and the Founding Fathers* of the United States later articulated this principle of "balanced government." In the nineteenth century, Alexis de Tocqueville* also stressed the tendency of popular democracies to succumb to the despotism* of demagogues*—political figures who manipulate the emotions of the masses for their own gain. Balanced government, by contrast, would provide a stable political foundation that preserved the safety and liberties of all citizens.

Calhoun's *Disquisition* informs a debate over the reach of America's central power that lasted from the 1787 ratification of the

Constitution* to the American Civil War*—a time frame known as the antebellum period.* On the one hand, proponents of Federalism* such as Alexander Hamilton,* John Adams,* and Daniel Webster* argued that the national government needed sufficient power to counter political majorities in individual states. But, on the other, opponents of Federalism, including Thomas Jefferson* and James Madison,* worried that this constitutional arrangement would lead to the tyranny of an elected majority.* Instead, these Anti-Federalists★ favored a union based on interdependence between equally sovereign states and a restricted central government.

The Contemporary Debate

In the 1840s and 1850s, Calhoun's works inspired proponents of the so-called "Calhoun Doctrine."* They argued that Congress** lacked the constitutional power to outlaw slavery in the southern states. But the Free Soil Party,* and later the Republican Party* vehemently opposed this view. They believed that the federal government and Congress *could* legally abolish slavery in the United States.

Calhounites cited the concept of the "concurrent majority," which was partly inspired, in its fears of majoritarian tyranny, by Anti-Federalists* such as Jefferson and Madison. Yet Calhoun went further than his predecessors in claiming that individual states had the constitutional right to veto laws enacted by a central government. *Disquisition* is one of the more radical defenses of the sovereignty of states in the American Republic.

Calhoun intended the concurrent majority as a constitutional solution to calm the sectional crises that racked the Union from the 1820s onwards. But had he lived after *Disquisition* was published, he would have witnessed how it had the opposite effect. After Calhoun died in 1850, members of the Democratic Party,* who represented the interests of slave-holding elites in the American South, rallied behind the concept of the concurrent majority to advocate for the secession of the southern states* from the Union. Drawing on Calhoun's ideas, these politicians argued that the only way to end the tyranny of the majoritarian government dominated by northern interests was to withdraw from the Union and dissolve the Republic. Seven southern states thus departed from the Union in 1861, sparking the American Civil War*—a bloody conflict that took the lives of 620,000 soldiers.

In his late-nineteenth-century biography of Calhoun, historian Herman Von Holst* argued that the "largest share of the responsibility for [the Civil War] rests on his [Calhoun's] shoulders."[4]

NOTES

1 John C. Calhoun, *A Disquisition on Government*, ed. H. Lee Cheek Jr. (South Bend, IN: St. Augustine's Press, 2007), 6.

2 John Adams, *A Defence of the Constitutions of Government of the United States of America*, Vol. 3 (London: 1788), 291.

3 Alexander Hamilton, John Jay, James Madison, and Isaac Kramnick (ed.), *The Federalist Papers* (Harmondsworth: Penguin Classics, 1987), Federalist Paper 10.

4 Herman Von Holst, *John C. Calhoun* (Boston: Houghton Mifflin Co., 1882), 350.

MODULE 4
THE AUTHOR'S CONTRIBUTION

KEY POINTS

- Calhoun argues that states rights' must be protected against the oppression of the federal (centralized) government.

- Calhoun seeks to safeguard slavery, without which the southern economy would suffer grave consequences.

- Calhoun's vision is rooted in previous political philosophy and is a product of contemporary tensions over the future of slavery and the power relationship between the federal and state governments.

Author's Aims

John C. Calhoun's *A Disquisition on Government* was aimed at statesmen and general readers who wanted to preserve the union between North and South, but who sympathized with the South's desire for political and economic freedom. Calhoun argued that because states made up the national government, each had the right to keep its interests free of federal meddling. Calhoun completed his text during a time of heightened political tension between the slave states in the South and the free states in the North. Following the Mexican–American War,* debate ensued as to whether the newly annexed territories would be slave or free. Calhoun hoped that *Disquisition* could provide a peaceful solution to the antagonisms between North and South; he never meant to inspire seven Southern states* to leave the Union in 1861.

Yet Calhoun always made it clear that all states had the right to secede—leave the Union—if they suffered oppression and tyranny. And so the text stirred up more friction than it eased. *Disquisition*

> ❝ In the *Disquisition*, Calhoun presented a theory of politics that is both original and in accord with the mainstream of the American political tradition. More than any other contemporary thinker of his period, Calhoun sought to explain the enduring qualities of American political thought in light of the troubled world of the mid-nineteenth century. ❞
>
> H. Lee Cheek Jr., *John C. Calhoun: Selected Writings and Speeches*

became a rallying point in the 1850s for proponents of the "Calhoun Doctrine,"* who argued that Congress* did not have the constitutional authority to abolish slavery in the American South. Calhoun's insistence on protecting states' rights stemmed from his determination to safeguard the practice of slavery. He knew that without slaves the southern economy would suffer.

Approach

Calhoun shared the central concept of *Disquisition*—the "concurrent majority"*—in a statement now known as the "Fort Hill Address." It was delivered in 1831 amidst heated debates over the constitutional right of individual states to nullify* federal legislation that harmed their economic interests. Calhoun's native state of South Carolina labored under federal tariffs* passed by Congress in the 1820s; this provoked widespread discontent and threats of secession* from the Union. And the growing strength of the anti-slavery abolitionist* movement in the North led to fears that the federal government would not only abolish slavery in the South, but also ruin its economic engine.

In the Fort Hill Address, Calhoun proposed that the Union could only survive when the various economic and social interests within the nation received proportional power. This expressed his concurrent majority concept in a nutshell. Calhoun also warned that the rising influence of a "numerical majority,"* through the central government's growing power, threatened the liberties of people within the United States.

As he put it: "The question of the relation which the States and General Government bear to each other is not one of recent origin. From the commencement of our system, it has divided public sentiment ... State-right, veto, nullification,* or by any other name—I conceive to be the fundamental principle of our system, resting on facts historically as certain as our revolution itself, and deductions as simple and demonstrative as that of any political, or moral truth whatever; and I firmly believe that on its recognition depend the stability and safety of our political institutions."[1]

Contribution in Context

Calhoun was, in fact, citing political questions that dated to 1776 and the founding of the United States. When the US Constitution* replaced the Articles of Confederation* in 1787, those same questions remained at stake. The Federalists* argued for its passing, while the Anti-Federalists* feared the prospect of a stronger federal government and the possibility that it would encroach on the power of the states. While the Constitution was a means to create a political union and national identity, the reality was that it had to be superimposed on already existing local and regional identities.

The tensions between federal and state power persisted throughout Calhoun's political career and helped to form his idea of a power-sharing concurrent majority. Following Calhoun's death in 1850, this concept profoundly influenced politics in the American South, especially amongst the states' rights* wing of the Democratic Party.* That is because it provided a useful tool for defending slavery against the abolitionist aims of federal politicians. Southern proponents of the concept of concurrent majority also warned that if the Congress ended slavery, it would overextend federal powers and violate the sovereignty and liberty of the southern states. Those same politicians and thinkers, also known as Calhounites, mobilized it as a constitutional defense of slavery—and ultimately as justification for southern states to split from the American Republic.

NOTES

1   John C. Calhoun, *The Fort Hill Address of July 26*, 1831 (Virginia: Virginia Commission on Constitutional Government, 1967).

SECTION 2
IDEAS

MODULE 5
MAIN IDEAS

KEY POINTS

- The three main themes of *A Disquisition on Government* are: human nature, the nature of government, and the role of a constitution* in federal government.

- The author's main argument is that minority rights must be protected against the oppression or tyranny of the majority.*

- Calhoun presents his three themes and main argument coherently in an effort to safeguard the practice of slavery and preserve the Union.

Key Themes

John C. Calhoun addresses three major themes in *A Disquisition on Government*. These are: the characteristics of humankind, the nature of government, and the role of a constitution in federal government.

Calhoun addresses the first theme by asserting that although man is a "social being," his individual feelings are more powerful than his social feelings.[1] This law of self-preservation dictates that individuals place their own interests over those of others, resulting in a "universal state of conflict, between individual and individual."[2]

The second theme of the text, the nature of government, follows from this description of the nature of humankind. For Calhoun, government is divinely ordained to allow men to live peaceably in the social state and act as a check on individual drives and passions. Without such a check, a community would otherwise plunge into anarchic* violence. But people, not divine powers, run governments. And, as such, Calhoun believes all forms of government (whether monarchical,* aristocratic,* or democratic*) tend to dominate people and abuse power.

> **❝** The Government of the absolute majority instead of
> the Government of the people is but the Government
> of the strongest interests; and when not efficiently
> checked, it is the most tyrannical and oppressive that
> can be devised. **❞**
>
> John C. Calhoun, cited in *Speeches of John C. Calhoun and Daniel Webster in the Senate of the United States on the Enforcing Bill*

In the third theme of the text, Calhoun argues that constitutional government* is a human contrivance, one required to "counteract the strong tendency of government to disorder and abuse." Calhoun considers a constitution as an "organism" to help the ruled resist the natural tendency of political rulers towards oppression and abuse of power.[3] To achieve this, the constitution must counteract any concentration of power, otherwise force would be the only means to resist abuses of power, plunging society into anarchy.*

These three themes form the foundations for Calhoun's discussion of an optimal constitutional arrangement. Nations need this, he argues, to preserve individual liberties against the tyranny of a political majority. Thus, the bulk of *Disquisition* is devoted to finding the ideal constitutional "organism"— one that would prevent a single group from dominating the entire community. For Calhoun, this is the "concurrent majority,"* a constitution that would grant power to "each interests or portion of the community"[4] to veto* or nullify* any law that threatened its interests. Calhoun sees this as the most perfect form of constitutional government—the only one that can contain deep-seated antagonisms among different community interests.

Exploring the Ideas

The text compares what Calhoun identifies as the two essential forms of government: "absolute" and "constitutional." Absolute government* —in whatever form—typically abuses power, which is concentrated in "one uncontrolled and irresponsible individual or body."[5] Unless this excessive concentration of government is stopped through constitutional checks, a ruling group will prevail over an entire community and create a tyranny of the "numerical majority,"* because this small group represents the majority of people who have voted for them.

In contrast, constitutional government harmonizes interests among social groups in a society.[6] This "harmony of interests" emerges by granting each interest group in a political society a negative check—through a right of veto (to stop a proposed law) or nullification (to invalidate a law it deems unconstitutional). Thus, minority groups can hold their ground against the competing interests of majority groups. Equal power will encourage compromise and give states a stable political foundation.

However, for Calhoun, "minority rights" refer specifically to the rights of propertied elites. Although the text avoids any explicit mention of slavery, he drafted the *Disquisition* to defend the rights of the South's slave-holding plantocracy* (the ruling class dominated by plantation owners). This group faced a threat from abolitionist* northern statesmen in the federal government.

As historian Richard Hofstadter* noted in 1948 in *The American Political Tradition*, the concurrent majority was a "device ... designed to protect a vested interest of considerable power. . . . it was minority privileges rather than minority rights that he really proposed to protect."[7] For Calhoun, "liberty" paradoxically includes the right to freely purchase and control the bodies of enslaved blacks. While Calhoun rails against tyrants in the "numerical majority," his *Disquisition* ironically supports despots in the plantocracy that he represented. Thus, Calhoun's reference to "minority rights" was never meant to apply to the rights of racial, ethnic, or religious minorities. Rather, his text works against them as it offers spirited support for the brutal, hegemonic* power of slave-holding elites.

Language and Expression

Calhoun writes clearly and concisely. He situates his argument in relation to previous political thought and key events of the times. He seeks to appeal to those who share his view that the North and South can compromise to preserve the political union of the United States.

At the same time, he is very cautious to avoid mentioning his underlying objective: to preserve slavery in the American South. Due to the great sensitivity of the subject, he addresses it in a roundabout way, framing his ideas through the lens of minority or states' rights. He proposes that individual states should be able to invalidate any law if they deemed it to be against their interests. While he never states this explicitly, this would include any central government law that freed slaves and, as a result, jeopardized the southern states' economy.

But Calhoun does not pull his arguments out of thin air. Rather they reflect the classical philosophy he learned as a youth, as well as the modern political thought of his era. Debates about the nature of political power date to Ancient Greece, and readers with this knowledge can readily relate Calhoun's arguments to the political thinkers that preceded him. That said, the author conveys his ideas and key concepts in a straightforward way without any dense language. Aside from the obvious fact that English has evolved since the document emerged in 1853, readers should find *Disquisition* easy to follow.

NOTES

1   John C. Calhoun, *A Disquisition on Government*, ed. H. Lee Cheek Jr. (South Bend, IN: St. Augustine's Press, 2007), 1.

2   Calhoun, *Disquisition on Government*, 3.

3   Calhoun, *Disquisition on Government*, 9.

4   Calhoun, *Disquisition on Government*, 21.

5   Calhoun, *Disquisition on Government*, 28.

6   Calhoun, *Disquisition on Government*, 19.

7   Richard Hofstadter, *The American Political Tradition and the Men who Made it* (New York: A. A. Knopf, 1948), 96.

MODULE 6
SECONDARY IDEAS

KEY POINTS

- For John C. Calhoun, government's fundamental goal is to improve the moral and intellectual faculties of mankind.

- The Enlightenment* shapes Calhoun's position on slavery. He argues that slavery is part of the "natural order" and a necessary step to make "barbarous peoples" (blacks) into "civilized beings."

- Calhoun argues that the development of technology and greater freedom of the press threatens to disrupt the existing social and political order of American society.

Other Ideas

John C. Calhoun's conception of "human progress" is a subordinate but nevertheless important element of his wider argument in *A Disquisition on Government*. Calhoun argues that the fundamental goal of government is to improve the moral and intellectual qualities of its people. For him, sound government lays the path to "progress, improvement and civilization"[1] by providing individuals with an optimal balance of protection and liberty. While the power of government protects society, the goal of liberty is "progress and the improvement of the human race."[2]

Calhoun believes that the political systems of the United States and United Kingdom represent mankind's most advanced and perfect governmental creations. To be sure, both have striking differences. America is a federal republic, or a federation of states based on the consent of the governed; Britain, by contrast, is a constitutional monarchy,* a system whereby a king or queen acts as the head of state

> **❝** Calhoun teaches that society originates in the nature of man, that it is original with man, and that the best kind of society is that which is most in accordance with the whole of human nature and which completes or perfects human nature. **❞**
>
> Guy Story Brown,* *Calhoun's Philosophy of Politics*

and an elected parliament drafts legislation. But Calhoun believes that, despite their distinctions, both of these systems offer the best possible checks against tyranny.

Exploring the Ideas

Calhoun's concept of progress has its roots in Enlightenment philosophies that sought to reform society through use of reason, and the theories of nineteenth-century social evolutionists.* In Calhoun's model of historical change, the transition from absolutist* to constitutional* government marks man's passage from a barbarous to a civilized state. And, as such, only a constitutional government* can safeguard the individual liberties needed for humanity to reach its full intellectual and moral potential.

But this does not apply to all humans. Calhoun believes that liberty belongs only to those who possess the necessary moral and intellectual faculties. To extend liberty to people sunk in "ignorance and vice" would "instead of a blessing, be a curse."[3] In this way, Calhoun maintains a contradictory position. On the one hand, liberty is necessary for human progress; on the other, it can only be granted to those already on a higher plane of civilization.

This squares with Calhoun's ideological justifications for enslaving blacks in the American South. He sees blacks as intellectually and morally inferior, needing the guidance and instruction of more-civilized segments of the population. Calhoun maintains that there was not a "punishment inflicted on the undeserving more just, than to be subject to lawless and despotic rule."[4] A slaveholder's despotism,* he believes, is necessary to aid the slow progress of barbarous peoples up the scale of civilization. To hasten their ascent on the "scale of liberty" would, according to Calhoun, disturb the natural order, creating "confusion," "disorder," and "anarchy."*

Overlooked

In *Disquisition*, Calhoun provides a brief, largely neglected analysis of how new technologies in information distribution—such as the steam engine, telegraph and steam-powered penny press*—were impacting contemporary politics. One benefit of these inventions, he argues, was "a great increase and diffusion of knowledge," which provided "an impulse to progress and civilization heretofore unexampled in the history of the world—accompanied by a mental energy and activity unprecedented."[5]

Yet Calhoun also worries about the increasing speed at which ideas, news, and opinions spread—rivaling "in rapidity, even thought itself."[6] His fear is that this might have a destabilizing effect on the social and political order. While champions of the free press proclaimed that it acted as a bulwark against the abuse of power, Calhoun warns that the press was becoming a tool for interest groups to manipulate public opinion, "moulding it, as to promote their peculiar interests."[7] As interest groups used this volatile "instrument of party warfare"[8] to vie for power, they threatened to create social and political anarchy by increasing "party excitement and the violence and virulence of party struggles."[9]

Calhoun's assessment of the penny press and its effect on American politics was far less optimistic than that of Alexis de Tocqueville,* who had remarked in his *Democracy in America* that newspapers "mend many more ills than they cause."[10] In many ways, Calhoun anticipates the works of twentieth-century critics such as Walter Lippmann* and

Noam Chomsky,* who harbored deep suspicions about how special interest groups could shape public opinion through mass media. Like these thinkers, Calhoun worries that the strongest interests in a society could come to manipulate public opinion through the press, and, as a result, impose tyranny.

Although *Disquisition* has long been criticized as overly abstract, Calhoun's discussion of the emerging print media and its impact on the democratic political process reveals that he could be an astute observer of contemporary sociopolitical developments.[11] His concerns apply just as much in today's Information Age as they did in the mid-nineteenth century, perhaps more so. Regardless, the media-politics connection outlined in Calhoun's text suggests a need to revisit and reinterpret it.

NOTES

1   John C. Calhoun, *A Disquisition on Government*, ed. H. Lee Cheek Jr. (South Bend, IN: St. Augustine's Press, 2007), 39.

2   Calhoun, *Disquisition on Government*, 41.

3   Calhoun, *Disquisition on Government*, 40–41.

4   Calhoun, *Disquisition on Government*, 42–43.

5   Calhoun, *Disquisition on Government*, 66–67.

6   Calhoun, *Disquisition on Government*, 66.

7   Calhoun, *Disquisition on Government*, 57.

8   Calhoun, *Disquisition on Government*, 57.

9   Calhoun, *Disquisition on Government*, 59.

10 Alexis de Tocqueville, *Democracy in America*, trans. Henry Reeve, vol. 2 (New York: Adlard and Saunders, 1838–40), 119.

11 H. Lee Cheek Jr., *Calhoun and Popular Rule: The Political Theory of the Disquisition and Discourse* (Columbia: University of Missouri Press, 2001), 24–27.

MODULE 7
ACHIEVEMENT

KEY POINTS

- Most progressive thinkers see Calhoun in a negative light due to his rejection of natural rights* and universal equality.*

- In defending states' rights,* Calhoun sought to safeguard the practice of slavery in the American South. He was ultimately unsuccessful.

- Nevertheless, his concepts of concurrent majority* and minority veto* remain relevant to contemporary political science. This is because, in different contexts, there are still worldwide concerns about the majority oppressing the minority.

Assessing the Argument

For modern readers, John C. Calhoun's rejection of natural rights and universal equality is perhaps the most jarring aspect of *A Disquisition on Government*. Today, these principles are considered essential. But in his text, Calhoun bemoans that the "prevalent opinion that men are born free and equal" is a ludicrous idea "destitute of all sound reason."[1] He maintains that men are born into a social and political order that demands submission to parental authority "under whose protection they draw their first breath."[2] The natural condition of man, in other words, is not of equality but rather of subordination backed up by the laws and institutions of the country. Calhoun asserts a "natural" social order where "the intelligent, the patriotic, the virtuous and deserving" rule over those who are "too ignorant, degraded, and vicious"—and incapable of "appreciating or of enjoying" liberty.[3]

By "ignorant, degraded and vicious," Calhoun means two groups: black slaves and, to a lesser extent, poor whites. His views not only fit his

❝ John C. Calhoun may be best known for his stature in the US Senate* and his controversial defense of slavery, but he is also a key figure in American political thought. The staunchest advocate of the consensus model of government as an alternative to majority rule,* he proposed government not by one, by few, or by many, but by all: each key group enjoying veto rights over collective decisions. **❞**

James. H. Read, *Majority Rule Versus Consensus: The Political Thought of John C. Calhoun*

broader defense of slavery, but they also counter the egalitarian claims of abolitionists* and liberal reformers in antebellum* America—the period between the formation of the American Republic and the American Civil War.*

In the years since *Disquisition*, however, the ideals of universal equality have become increasingly widespread—and this has damaged Calhoun's legacy and reputation. Criticism of his works began as early as the waning days of the American Civil War, when anti-slavery writers condemned the *Disquisition* for backing the "doomed and unholy cause" of slavery.[4]

And in the twentieth century, Calhoun's implicit justification of white racial supremacy discredited his entire body of thought—especially during the horrors of racial genocide* under the Nazi* regime in World War II.* After that war, progressive and liberal thinkers came of age witnessing the signing of the Universal Declaration of Human Rights* and the Civil Rights Movement* of the 1960s—a challenge to America's anti-black laws and policies—so their thinking was very much at odds with Calhoun's.

As racial justice and social equality came to dominate American politics, interpretations of *Disquisition* focused on how it supported the racist and elitist politics of the antebellum South. Liberal thinkers Richard Hofstadter,*

Richard N. Current,* and Louis Hartz* were its most prominent critics. They vehemently denied that *Disquisition* contained any principles of universal value or enduring worth and maintained that it could not be read without addressing the author's support of slavery. Because Calhoun defends the morally indefensible institution of slavery, his text has been largely excluded from the canon of American political thought.

Achievement in Context

That said, *Disquisition* can also be seen as a last-ditch (and ultimately futile) attempt to save the United States from civil war through political reform that would more fully protect the interests of individual states within the federation. Calhoun writes in *Disquisition* that one great advantage of a "concurrent majority"* was its "disposition to harmonize."[5] Calhoun saw the overextension of power by a "majority government"* in Washington as the cause of contemporary political disorder. As a result, he seeks a more conciliatory political structure to stabilize the Union by giving greater weight to minority groups and interests—specifically the plantocracy* of the South that he represents.

Calhoun's achievement was to extend this classical analysis of politics to nineteenth-century America. He believed that the United States was slowly falling prey to the despotism* of a "numerical majority"* that advanced its own interests through complete control over the chambers of government. *Disquisition* was an attempt to develop a "proper organism"[6] (or constitutional structure) of government that could more equitably distribute political power and address the diverse needs and interests of social groups within the society. Only a concurrent majority* that would grant veto* powers to minority groups* under a majority government could curb excesses of power.

Limitations

Disquisition steers clear of discussing the social and political context of its time, and this hinders current attempts to understand it. To appreciate Calhoun's intentions, one must read the text as the culmination of a nuanced political career. For while he acted as a staunch advocate of the sovereignty of southern states, Calhoun was also a conciliatory figure who tried to prevent the collapse of the American Republic. What's more, one must understand that debates about the relationship between the federal government and the states, and the fear of tyranny, date back to America's separation from Britain in 1776—when the Thirteen Colonies* rebelled against an abusive monarchy.* Thus, *Disquisition* was part of a longer-standing debate and tension regarding the scope and function of government.

Another impediment to understanding the text is that Calhoun never explicitly mentions his views on slavery or his desire to safeguard its practice. As a result, anyone unaware of *Disquisition*'s historical context would miss the underlying argument behind the whole work. Furthermore, since Calhoun defends "minority rights"—meaning states' rights*—one could even assume that he *supports* natural rights and universal equality. But this is in absolute contradiction to what he actually believed. Calhoun did not sympathize with the minority rights of racial minorities or slaves, but rather the minority rights of an exclusive southern plantocracy of privileged slave owners.

NOTES

1   John C. Calhoun, *A Disquisition on Government*, ed. H. Lee Cheek Jr. (South Bend, IN: St. Augustine's Press, 2007), 43.

2   Calhoun, *Disquisition on Government*, 44.

3   Calhoun, *Disquisition on Government*, 41–42.

4   Daniel Feller, "John C. Calhoun," in *Reader's Guide to American History*, ed. Peter J. Parish (Chicago: Fitzroy Dearborn Publishers, 1997), 89.

5   Calhoun, *Disquisition on Government*, 50.

6   Calhoun, *Disquisition on Government*, 19.

MODULE 8
PLACE IN THE AUTHOR'S WORK

KEY POINTS

- John C. Calhoun's body of work sought to protect states' rights* and interests* under majority rule.*

- This body of work was coherent, and *A Disquisition on Government* was its high point.

- *Disquisition* cemented Calhoun's positive legacy as a defender of states' rights against majority oppression, as well as his negative legacy as a staunch advocate of the practice of slavery.

Positioning

A Disquisition on Government was the culmination of a long career during which John C. Calhoun championed the protection of states' rights and interests. The core ideas of *Disquisition* trace back to Calhoun's earliest publication, "Exposition and Protest," drafted in 1828 at the request of the South Carolina legislature.* This text was secretly published during the "Nullification Crisis"* of 1832–33, sparked by South Carolina's threat to invalidate federal tariffs* within its territory. "Exposition and Protest" defended the rights of states to veto* federal laws detrimental to the interests of states and their people within the federation.

In 1831, Calhoun published the "Fort Hill Address," which hints at his later critique of majority rule. In "Fort Hill," he first coined the central concept of *Disquisition*: the "concurrent majority,"* whereby unanimous agreement among states formed a basis for fair government.

In the 1830s and 1840s, Calhoun published a number of tracts—notably the 1849 "Southern Address"—in which he provided a constitutional defense of the institution of slavery. That defense came amidst fears that a

> **❝** Calhoun's political and philosophical thought evolved over a forty-year period of public office ... In general language, he sought practical solutions to designed to alleviate the tensions under which the American system labored. His systematic theory about the nature of man and government ... deserves careful attention for his part in the ongoing discussion of the uneasy, but critical, relationship between liberty and union. **❞**
>
> Ross M. Lence* (ed.), foreword to *Union and Liberty*

majority government* in Washington, driven by northern abolitionist* interests, would end slavery in the southern states.* In this way, *Disquisition* distills the life's work of a statesman who fought to protect the economic and political interests of southern slave owners.

Integration

Disquisition's central theme—the increasing threat that the "tyranny of the majority*" posed to individual liberty—places the work within the tradition of classical republican* political philosophy. In this political tradition, pure democracies* are regarded as naturally unstable, prone to give way to the anarchy* of party conflict and excessive concentration of political power. The solution to this deep-rooted problem with the structure of popular democracies—to distribute political power among states in a nation—links the text to the school of Jeffersonian republicanism.*

The distribution of political powers between the federal government and the states had been a subject of considerable political debate and ideological conflict since the American Revolution.* Thomas Jefferson,* the principal author of the Declaration of Independence* and third president of the United States, tried to ensure a right of states to veto* laws passed by Congress* that were believed to constitute an abuse of powers.

That was influential for later supporters of states' rights* like Calhoun. The *Disquisition* follows in this Jeffersonian tradition in proposing a constitutional arrangement to protect the rights of minority groups* within a majority government* by giving them the right to nullify laws seen to infringe on their interests.

Significance

Calhoun's growing fear that the economic and political interests of the southern states were being trampled in a nation increasingly dominated by northern interests, including the anti-slavery movement, drove his theoretical reflections in *Disquisition*. Statesmen in the American South, in contrast, were seeking to preserve the interests of the plantation economies, but many also hoped to maintain the integrity of the Union. Thus, Calhoun proposed a constitutional structure that would protect the separate interests and liberties of individual states while preserving the larger Union.

Yet despite his efforts to keep the United States intact, Calhoun's reputation suffered greatly following the end of the American Civil War* and the abolition of slavery. In the late nineteenth and twentieth century, he came to be seen as a "philosopher of reaction,"[1] to use the historian Richard N. Current's* term—one who had devoted his life to defending a morally indefensible institution. Nevertheless, political scientists, such as Arthur M. Schlesinger Jr.* and Peter F. Drucker,* have asserted that Calhoun's concept of the concurrent majority remains relevant for the study of modern politics and argue that it can be separated analytically from his support of slavery.[2]

NOTES

1   Richard N. Current, "John C. Calhoun, Philosopher of Reaction," *Antioch Review 3* (1943): 225.

2   For further details, see: Arthur M. Schlesinger Jr., *The Age of Jackson* (Boston: Little, Brown and Company,1945); Peter F. Drucker, "A Key to American Politics: Calhoun's Pluralism," *Review of Politics 10* (1948): 412–26.

SECTION 3
IMPACT

MODULE 9
THE FIRST RESPONSES

KEY POINTS

- National leaders such as James Madison* and Daniel Webster*—who advocated a strong central government as outlined in the US Constitution*—heavily criticized *Disquisition* upon its publication.

- Since *Disquisition* was published posthumously, Calhoun did not respond to his critics. Nevertheless, the text was a continuation of his previous writings, which also staunchly defended states' rights* and the practice of slavery.

- The most important factors that shaped the work's reception were the forceful debates of the time between those who favored a strong central government and those who defended states' rights, and between those who defended slavery and those who wished to abolish it.

Criticism

John C. Calhoun's concept of a "concurrent majority"* as outlined in *A Disquisition on Government* attracted a great deal of criticism from his contemporaries. Nationalists* and Neo-Federalists* like Daniel Webster* opposed the doctrine from the 1830s onwards. But it's important to note that those groups represented the interests of northern commercial elites who wanted to harness central government to spur economic development. Webster waged a lifelong campaign against Calhoun's defense of states' rights* and backed the undivided sovereignty of the national government.

Webster and the Neo-Federalists believed that the concurrent majority concept not only violated the American Constitution,* but it was also unworkable. In *Disquisition,* Calhoun had argued that

> **❝** Throughout *A Disquisition on Government*, there is an inherent, though never expressed, argument for the perpetuation of slavery, concealed behind the façade of minority rights. **❞**
>
> John Nevin, *John C. Calhoun and the Price of Union*

under a concurrent majority, a majority government* would be checked, as all minority groups and interests could exercise the right of veto.* This led Webster and his fellow critics to reply that this constitutional arrangement would provoke political paralysis and plunge the United States into anarchy.* For Webster, a concurrent majority would restrict the power of central government to the point of political deadlock.

Calhoun's most illustrious critic was James Madison,* who refuted the idea of states' rights—even though he had championed them in the Virginia Report* of 1800. In that text, Madison claimed that because states were "parties to the constitutional compact," there could be "no tribunal above their authority."[1] Yet towards the end of his life, Madison rejected Calhoun's claim that individual states possessed the right to nullify* laws enacted by Congress.* Such a principle, he wrote, was "pregnant with consequences subversive of the Constitution."[2] Instead, Madison proposed a "divided sovereignty," which denied that any individual political body—either at the federal or state level—had ultimate authority over constitutional questions. Madison's dismissal of unilateral nullification,* coming as it did from the last of the Founding Fathers,* carried great weight and discredited Calhoun's idea of concurrent majority.

Responses

In the end, Calhoun never had the chance to respond to his critics: *Disquisition* was published just after his death in 1851. Yet Calhoun did address objections to the idea of concurrent majority that dated back two decades to the presidency of Andrew Jackson.* The most serious of those objections was that it was impractical. Under a concurrent majority, all minority groups* could veto* or nullify* legislation passed by a majority government.* As a result, they would hold a dangerous power: to hamper government operations and create stalemate.

In *Disquisition*, Calhoun accepts that a government founded on the principle of the concurrent majority might seem "too slow in its movements and too weak in its foundations to succeed in practice."[3] Yet he also suggests that this arrangement would produce compromise rather than stalemate. The "urgent necessity to unite on some common course of action," he writes, would lead political leaders to cooperate in order to avoid the "convulsions and anarchy"* that would ensue from a deadlocked government.[4] The need for unanimous agreement among diverse interest groups within a society would not produce a weak government, but rather one that would "promote the common interests of the whole."[5] By forcing political compromise, the concurrent majority would harmonize conflicting concerns, "impelling all to acquiesce in whatever the common good requires."[6]

Calhoun presents historical examples to back his claims. A legislative body in which all members could veto proceedings ruled the Kingdom of Poland,* he writes, and this formed the source of its "great power and splendor." Then he cites the Confederacy of the Six Nations,* a group of Native American tribes in New York State in which council members could veto proposals relating to common welfare. This, he writes, "secured harmony in council and action, and with them a great increase of power."[7] In this way, Calhoun refutes that a concurrent majority weakens the ability of statesmen to govern. Instead, he argues that it greatly strengthens the power of a state.

Conflict and Consensus

Liberal thinkers* criticized *Disquisition* following World War II.*
Historians Richard Hofstadter* and Richard N. Current,* as well as
political scientist Louis Hartz,* spurned the treatise and, as a result,
influenced post-war scholars of American political philosophy. They
viewed *Disquisition* as an aberration within the American political
tradition, which they understood as progressively evolving towards
greater equality and individual liberty. Calhoun, in their
understanding, was a "philosopher of reaction,"[8] and *Disquisition* was
the nineteenth century's most powerful argument for the privileges
and brutal power of the southern plantocracy.*

Hofstadter expressed this view when he concluded that the
concurrent majority was a "device ... designed to protect a vested
interest of considerable power ... it was minority privileges rather than
minority rights that he really proposed to protect."[9] In his interpretation,
Disquisition stands as a profoundly conservative work of political
philosophy with a single aim: to protect southern elites against the
egalitarian aims of anti-slavery abolitionists* and liberal reformers.

This criticism effectively pushed *Disquisition* into the margins of
the American political tradition. However, scholars in recent decades
have reinterpreted it as not simply a pro-slavery text, but also a
treatise that contributed to nineteenth and twentieth century
political thought. H. Lee Cheek Jr.* has argued that *Disquisition*
must be seen as part of a distinctive brand of "South Atlantic"
republicanism that sought to curb the excesses of popular rule and
limit the power of the central government over states within the
Union.[10] In fact, Cheek believes that Calhoun's work provokes a
broader debate about the nature of political power in popular
democracies—an important issue not just in Calhoun's time or
today. The abuse of majority power has concerned American
politicians ever since the United States left British rule.

NOTES

1   James Madison, "The Report of 1800," January 7th 1800, in *Papers of James Madison*, ed. W. T. Hutchinson et al. (Chicago: University of Chicago Press, c.1962), 17: 309–10. Cited in William K. Bolt, "Founding Father and Rebellious Son: James Madison, John C. Calhoun and the Use of Precedents," *American Nineteenth-Century History 5*, no. 3 (2004): 13.

2   James Madison to Robert Y. Hayne, April 3rd or 4th, 1830, in Gaillard Hunt, ed., *The Writings of James Madison* (New York and London: G. P. Putnam's Sons, 1900–10), 9: 390. Cited in Bolt, "Founding Father and Rebellious Son," 15–16.

3   John C. Calhoun, *A Disquisition on Government*, ed. H. Lee Cheek Jr. (South Bend, IN: St. Augustine's Press, 2007), 48.

4   Calhoun, *Disquisition on Government*, 50.

5   Calhoun, *Disquisition on Government*, 52.

6   Calhoun, *Disquisition on Government*, 53.

7   Calhoun, *Disquisition on Government*, 55.

8   Richard N. Current, "John C. Calhoun, Philosopher of Reaction," *Antioch Review 3* (1943):   225.

9   Richard Hofstadter, *The American Political Tradition and the Men Who Made It* (New York: A. A. Knopf), 96.

10 H. Lee Cheek Jr., *Calhoun and Popular Rule: The Political Theory of the Disquisition and Discourse* (Columbia: University of Missouri Press, 2001), 10.

MODULE 10
THE EVOLVING DEBATE

KEY POINTS

- John C. Calhoun's core concepts—concurrent majority*
  and minority veto*—are seminal in political science.

- Calhoun is remembered for two things: defending slavery
  and defending states' rights* against majority oppression.

- Since World War II,* Calhoun's ideas have been revitalized
  for the support of minority rights.*

Uses and Problems

John C. Calhoun's *A Disquisition on Government* was dismissed as
irrelevant in the years after the American Civil War.* The "concurrent
majority" concept became inescapably linked with Calhoun's pro-
slavery views, and was further undermined following abolition.

But since the end of World War II, political scientists have
increasingly argued the relevance of the concurrent majority in
modern democratic politics. In 1945, historian Arthur M. Schlesinger
Jr.* stated that Calhoun's concept could be of value to any minority
group, not simply a nineteenth century slave-holding minority in the
South. Schlesinger suggested that people could apply Calhoun's ideas
to progressive causes, though this would demand a radical departure
from the original intentions of the text.

African American political scientist Hanes Walton Jr.* also
argued that the concurrent majority could be "relevant in a
corrective, creative, and useful way to Black Revolution." In his 1971
book, *Political Philosophy of Martin Luther King*, Walton maintained
that Calhoun's "powerful statement of the rights of minorities …
against the tyranny of the majority"* could mobilize African

> **" Calhoun was in fact a seminal political thinker who spoke not only to his time and place, but also to the modern world .... He had a coherent, systematic view of human nature and society made a lasting contribution to constitutional and democratic theory. "**
>
> H. Lee Cheek Jr., *Calhoun and Popular Rule*

Americans to demand a right of veto* on public policy issues affecting their interests.[1] The paradox of using Calhoun this way was not lost on Walton, who remarked that it would be "the height of irony if the arguments advanced ... by the most gifted and influential apologist for black enslavement were converted ... into arguments for black liberation."[2]

One has to wonder what Calhoun—a slavery apologist—would think of racial minorities using his *Disquisition* as a rallying point. Historian Richard N. Current* objected to this interpretation, disputing the idea that "the case for the one-time master can be converted into a case for the one-time slave."[3]

Yet modern consensus amongst historians and political scientists is that concurrent majority is far more adaptable than Current allows. Most recently, H. Lee Cheek Jr.* has argued that "Current's unusual presentation of Calhoun as an obstacle ... to the rights of minorities in our own day shows a reluctance to consider the diversity and depth of Calhoun's political thought ... the use of Calhoun's theory by minority groups continues, and has experienced a revival in recent years, encouraging the need for a thorough presentation of Calhoun's thought."[4]

Schools of Thought

After nearly a century of neglect, "neo-Calhounians" in the second half of the twentieth century have used *Disquisition*'s ideas to advance the aims of a pluralist democracy* where multiple parties share power. The historian Arthur M. Schlesinger Jr. first called for a rehabilitation of Calhoun's thought in 1945, finding in *Disquisition* a "brilliant and penetrating study of modern society, whose insights remain vital for any minority."[5] In the 1960s, neo-Calhounians primarily drawn from the political left, began to assemble around the concept of the concurrent majority. The American political scientist Darryl Baskin,* for instance, found in *Disquisition* "a pluralist vision … a way of looking at things political that is congenial to our … anti-majoritarian mode of political life."[6]

At the same time, civil rights* activists began to argue that *Disquisition* contained useful insights for building a political system that would respect the rights and interests of African Americans and other racial minorities. Following on from the argument of Hanes Walton Jr.* that African Americans could use Calhoun's tyranny of the majority reasoning to demand a right to veto on public policy that was against their interests, legal scholar Lani Guinier* has argued that an electoral system based on concurrent majority would better protect racial minorities in the United States. In her 1994 book, *The Tyranny of the Majority: Fundamental Fairness in Representative Democracy*, Guinier drew inspiration from Calhoun's *Disquisition* to offer a critique of a majoritarian government dominated by the interests of white Americans.

Thus, these scholars have transposed Calhoun's basic argument to a twentieth-century context. *Disquisition* has provided a springboard for thinking about how racial minorities and their interests can be protected under democratically elected majority governments.*

This modern application is, however, profoundly at odds with Calhoun's original intent. Far from seeking to defend the rights of racial minorities, Calhoun formulated the concept to protect the institution of slavery and the minority interests of the slave-holding elite in the American South. However, neo-Calhounians defend this "reassociation of ideas and purpose,"[7] arguing that Calhoun's thought contains insights "of perennial interest to Americans and the world."[8]

In Current Scholarship

In the spirit of *Disquisition*, neo-Calhounian thinkers believe that potential tyranny by elected majorities demands a political system that guarantees political influence to minority groups* within society. Lani Guinier,* for instance, recently enlisted the idea of a concurrent majority in developing new electoral schemes that would grant greater legislative power and representation to African Americans.

Current proponents of Calhoun's thought have also grappled with the fact that Calhoun was one of the most prominent champions of slavery and racial apartheid* in the American South. He was long derided as a "philosopher of reaction" by scholars who rightly condemned him for providing an intellectual and constitutional defense of slavery.[9] But those who've revived discussion of *Disquisition* argue against dismissing Calhoun as a supporter of slavery and nothing more. Cheek has maintained that the "philosophical and historical questions Calhoun pondered are of perennial interest to Americans and the world." In his 2001 book, *Calhoun and Popular Rule: The Political Theory of the Disquisition and Discourse,* he argues that Calhoun was a "seminal political thinker" whose insights into democratic government and the protection of minority rights remain relevant for the modern world.[10]

Yet such views may very well minimize how slavery and racism influenced Calhoun's political philosophy. Neo-Calhounians have demonstrated that the ideas developed in *Disquisition* can help stimulate a more pluralist form of politics. But an accurate, unflinching view of the text must firmly place the work within its historical context: the pro-slavery politics of the American South that Calhoun supported without reservation.

NOTES

1   Cited in Vukan Kuic, "John C. Calhoun's Theory of the Concurrent Majority," *American Bar Association Journal* 69 (1983): 485.

2   Cited in Kuic, "Calhoun's Theory of the Concurrent Majority," 485.

3   Richard N. Current, *John C. Calhoun* (New York: Washington Square Press, 1963), 234.

4   H. Lee Cheek Jr., *Calhoun and Popular Rule: The Political Theory of the Disquisition and Discourse* (Columbia: University of Missouri Press, 1963), 22.

5   Arthur M. Schelsinger Jr., *The Age of Jackson* (Boston: Little, Brown and Company, 1945), 405.

6   Darryl Baskin, "The Pluralist Vision of John C. Calhoun," *Polity* 2, no. 1 (1969): 50.

7   Stephen Skowronek, "The Reassociation of Ideas and Purposes: Racism, Liberalism and the American Political Tradition," *American Political Science Review* 100, no. 3 (2006): 385–401.

8   Cheek, Jr., *Calhoun and Popular Rule*, 13.

9   Richard N. Current, "John C. Calhoun, Philosopher of Reaction," *Antioch Review* 3 (1943): 225.

10 Cheek, Jr., *Calhoun and Popular Rule*, ix.

MODULE 11
IMPACT AND INFLUENCE TODAY

KEY POINTS

- *A Disquisition on Government* is a seminal text in political science.
- Although John C. Calhoun's position on slavery has been heavily scrutinized, his core concept, the concurrent majority,* remains an important one among modern scholars.
- The text has the greatest modern value in relation to pluralist democracy* and minority rights.*

Position

In the late twentieth century, two US Supreme Court* decisions upheld John C. Calhoun's principle of the "concurrent majority" as consistent with the democratic principles of the American Constitution.* In the 1970s, a lower court struck down a New York law that required county charters to be approved by "separate majorities of voters residing in cities and outside of cities."[1] However, the Supreme Court upheld the law in 1977, citing a "concurrent majority requirement, which recognizes discrete interests that local units of government may have."[2] The ruling in the case (*Town of Lockport v. Citizens for Community Action at the Local Level*) thus explicitly invoked Calhoun's concurrent majority concept in protecting the public interest.

In 1982, the Supreme Court again cited concurrent majority, this time in *Rogers v. Lodge*. The court deemed that politicians elected by a white-voter majority in Burke County, Georgia systematically ignored the interests of African Americans. The court ruled that if voting procedures for the county board of commissioners were aligned on the

> 66 Posterity decided against Calhoun's argument for the
> indefinite protection of slavery ....What he had to say
> about the need in popular governments like our own to
> protect the rights of minorities, about the importance of
> choosing leaders with character, talent, and the willingness
> to speak hard truths to the people, and about the enduring
> need ... for the people themselves to develop and sustain
> both the civic culture and the institutional structures
> which contribute to their lasting interest is as fresh and
> significant today as it was in 1850. 99
>
> Irving H. Bartlett,* *John C. Calhoun: A Biography*

principle of the concurrent majority, "minority candidates would not lose elections solely because of their race." Thus both the *Lockport* and *Rogers* cases demonstrated that the concurrent majority concept held the key to a fairer, more equitable form of democratic politics—and made a real, noticeable impact on the procedures of government.[3] These examples point to the enduring importance of *A Disquisition on Government* in political science.

Interaction

Modern political scientists have noted how Calhoun's *Disquisition* has exerted a surprising influence in international relations.* Two years after the formation of the United Nations,* American political scientist Mitchell Franklin* remarked that this organization reflected Calhoun's concept of the concurrent majority. The architects of the United Nations, for example, gave veto* power to permanent members of the Security Council.*

Political scientists Ronnie W. Faulkner* and Michael M. Gunter* likewise argued that the Security Council's veto is "the supreme manifestation of Calhoun's theory of the 'concurrent majority.'" In the

1980s, Faulkner and Gunter went so far as to compare the United States' minority position in the United Nations to that of the American South prior to the Civil War.* Just as Calhoun warned of the growing tyranny of a majority government* dominated by northern interests, Faulkner and Gunter remarked that the UN's General Assembly* had a "Third World majority that displays all the tendencies towards abuse of power." They also called for the United States to use its Security Council veto power more frequently, noting that these were the "demands of international reality" and "the imperatives of the Calhoun philosophy."[4]

Political scientists have also noted the relevance of Calhoun's ideas for promoting peace in countries hampered by sectional conflict and civil war. Arend Lijphart's* concept of "consociational democracy,"* for instance, was inspired by Calhoun's concurrent majority concept. For Lijphart, a concurrent majority represents a more viable form of political organization in "culturally and ethnically divided societies" because it protects minority groups from majority government tyranny. In countries such as South Africa, where a numerical minority* imposed apartheid* on racial and ethnic majorities, concurrent majority "offers the only realistic possibility to attain a viable democratic system."[5]

The Continuing Debate

Attempts in the 1950s to rehabilitate *Disquisition* as a means to defend racial and ethnic minorities have not gone unchallenged. Civil War* historian Richard N. Current* believed *Disquisition* was inherently racist; he opposed how mid-century liberals tried to shift its purpose. Pointing to leaders of the Civil Rights movement,* Current refused to believe that the "the case for the one-time master can be converted into a case for the one-time slave."[6] In fact, Current found it utterly perverse that the nineteenth century's staunchest supporter of slavery could be drafted to fight racial inequality. The authentic "spirit of Calhoun," he wrote, lived on in the "White Citizens Council of Mississippi" that sought to protect racial apartheid against the efforts of civil rights activists.

While Current used liberal principles to challenge "neo-Calhounians," other criticisms have come from the opposite end of the ideological spectrum. When legal scholar and civil rights activist Lani Guinier* proposed an American electoral system based on the concurrent majority, conservative commenters fired back. The British Conservative John O'Sullivan,* for example, blasted Guinier's attempt to revive Calhoun's concepts and "fancy franchises" as destructive to the cohesiveness of American society. By making ethnic groups the "building blocks of political society," he charged, Guinier was laying "the [groundwork] for low-intensity civil wars."[7] Like Current, O'Sullivan finds fault with applying concurrent majority in modern politics. But unlike Current, he believes that modern liberal thought and Calhoun's conservatism do not conflict. He sees a destructive tendency in both that threatens anarchy* by splitting society into separate interest groups. It's a fascinating conclusion, given that Calhoun sought to preserve the Union through his text.

NOTES

1   Vukan Kuic, "John C. Calhoun's Theory of the Concurrent Majority," *American Bar Association Journal* 69 (1983): 485.

2   Kuic, "Calhoun's Theory of the Concurrent Majority," 485.

3   Kuic, "Calhoun's Theory of the Concurrent Majority," 485.

4   Ronnie W. Faulkner and Michael M. Gunter, "UN Ambassador Daniel Patrick Moynihan and the Calhounian Connection," *Teaching Political Science: Politics in Perspective* 13, no.2 (1986): 71.

5   Arend Lijphart, "Majority rule versus democracy in deeply divided societies," *Politikon: South African Journal of Political Studies* 4 (1977): 113–26.

6   Richard N. Current, *John C. Calhoun* (New York: Washington Square Press, 1963), 234.

7   John O' Sullivan, "Mistaken Identities," *National Review* 48, no. 22 (1996): 56.

MODULE 12
WHERE NEXT?

KEY POINTS

- Since World War II,* there has been renewed interest in *Disquisition.*
- *Disquisition* will very likely continue to shape debates on pluralist democracy* and minority rights.*
- The text is seminal because for over a century and a half it has influenced debates and scholarship in the field of political science.

Potential

For nearly a century after it was published, profound historical changes rendered John C. Calhoun's *A Disquisition on Government* obsolete. The text was deemed irrelevant following the South's defeat in the American Civil War* in 1865 because it defended the "minority rights" of slaveholders in the American South. For many people, Calhoun's concept of the "concurrent majority*"—championed in the antebellum* period between the founding of the American Republic and the Civil War by defenders of slavery—was simply the relic of a bygone era. Just two years after *Disquisition* was published in 1851, President Abraham Lincoln* freed America's slaves. So, at best, Calhoun's thought could have only endured in the minds of racist extremists.

Since the Holocaust,* however, the text has been revitalized in support of oppressed minorities. In the 1960s, it became particularly relevant when African Americans struggled for equal civil rights.* And in the years since, various people have evoked it to highlight the importance of a pluralist democracy* (where multiple parties share

> ❝ Calhoun's understanding of the need for ethical-political restraint and for institutional means for obtaining concurrence is especially relevant to the present situation in the Western world, marked as it is by growing ethnic and cultural conflict and social fragmentation. ❞
>
> H. Lee Cheek Jr.,* *Calhoun and Popular Rule*

power) and the interests of minorities.

 Yet Calhoun's influence in these areas will probably not stop there. The United States is but one example of a system in which tension exists between the central government and sub-national entities. The same pressures are found in Belgium, Canada, Iraq, Spain, and the United Kingdom, where, respectively, Flanders, Quebec, Kurdistan, Catalonia, and Scotland engage in continual negotiation to further minority interests and expand their autonomy. And in the European Union,* power struggles have pitted smaller states such as Greece against larger, more powerful states such as Germany. Calhoun's arguments can applied to these examples and others.

Future Directions
One of the most prominent current proponents of Calhoun's thought is H. Lee Cheek Jr.,* dean of social sciences and professor of political science at East Georgia College. He maintains that the "philosophical and historical questions Calhoun pondered are of perennial interest to Americans and the World."[1] For Cheek, *Disquisition* cannot be shrugged off as a simple pro-slavery document.

In fact, Cheek maintains that Calhoun's concerns with "liberty, freedom, equality, sovereignty, [and] popular rule"[2] lie at the heart of the modern American political tradition. And as the political scientist Stephen Skowronek* has remarked, the recent appropriation of

Calhoun's ideas by liberal thinkers demonstrates the flexibility of the American political tradition. "By reassociating ideas and purposes over deep cultural divides, political actors are apt to articulate principles with meanings of their own, to elaborate through ideas culturally distinctive senses of purpose."[3] Thus, the inclusion of Calhounian thought in today's liberal American political tradition ensures *Disquisition's* lasting relevance.

In the future, Calhoun's concept of a concurrent majority* will most likely continue to influence debates on how to achieve balance between national and sub-national governments. His strong support of minority rights also applies to any context where majorities oppress smaller groups, as with issues of gender, ethnicity, religion, and sexual orientation.

Summary

John C. Calhoun's *A Disquisition on Government* is one of the seminal texts of nineteenth-century American political thought. Calhoun critiques the tyrannical tendencies of "majority government"* and sees them as the inherent defect of a democracy. Calhoun addresses this with his concept of the concurrent majority—a form of government that gives minority interest groups the power to veto* majority legislation and thus prevent tyranny.

Calhoun developed his concurrent majority concept amidst great political tension between free states in the northern United States and slave states in the American South. *Disquisition* was intended to provide a defense of slaveholders in the American South and their economic interest. Calhoun saw the South as suffering under the tyranny of a federal government dominated by northern interests.

Because *Disquisition* supported the racist politics of the American South, the text, and Calhoun's thought in general, fell into disrepute following the American Civil War.* But after nearly a century of neglect, *Disquisition* was rehabilitated in the second half of the twentieth century by liberal thinkers who found it useful for debates on pluralist democracy and minority rights. In recent decades, politicians have invoked the concept of the concurrent majority, claiming that it holds the key to a fairer form of democratic politics. And today, Calhoun's continuing impact has spurred recent calls by historians and political scientists such as H. Lee Cheek Jr.* for a deeper analysis of *Disquisition*.

Taken at face value, Calhoun's text merely serves to bolster the racist policy of slavery. Yet a thorough study of *A Disquisition on Government* also reveals John C. Calhoun as a distinguished politician who tried to keep a threatened Union intact by giving voice to minority interests. That notion of voice, expressed through Calhoun's concurrent majority, gives hope to oppressed minorities today and has rescued his reputation as an original political thinker.

NOTES

1   H. Lee Cheek Jr., *Calhoun and Popular Rule: The Political Theory of the Disquisition and Discourse* (Columbia: University of Missouri Press, 1963), ix.

2   Cheek Jr., *Calhoun and Popular Rule*, 13.

3   Skowronek, "The Reassociation of Ideas and Purposes: Racism, Liberalism and American Political Tradition," *American Political Science Review* 100, no.2 (2006): 387.

GLOSSARY

GLOSSARY OF TERMS

Abolitionism: a movement to end slavery that began in Britain in the late eighteenth century and gained popularity in the United States in the early nineteenth century. John C. Calhoun's *A Disquisition on Government* argued that the practice of slavery was part of the "natural order" and should continue.

Absolutist government: a political system in which a single ruler is not constrained by laws or legally recognized opposition. This was the system in European countries prior to the Glorious Revolution in England in 1688 and the French Revolution of 1789.

American Civil War (1861–5): an armed conflict between the slave-owning states of the American South and the northern states, sparked by the secession of seven southern states in 1861. Contrary to its purpose, Calhoun's *Disquisition* helped inspire this split.

American Constitution: a document adopted in 1787 and ratified in 1789 that acts as the supreme law of the United States of America.

American Revolution: a political upheaval in the late eighteenth century that saw the Thirteen Colonies revolt against the British Empire and establish the United States of America. The central debate in Calhoun's *Disquisition* regarding the proper role of government and the potential of a "tyranny of the majority" dates to this period.

Anarchy: a political state of lawlessness and lack of centralized authority. In *Disquisition*, Calhoun argued that abolishing slavery would disrupt the "natural order" and result in anarchy.

Antebellum: the period following the foundation of the American

Republic until the American Civil War. Calhoun's *Disquisition* was published during this period in 1851.

Anti-Federalism: a movement in late eighteenth-century and nineteenth-century American politics that opposed a strong federal government. Calhoun's *Disquisition* fits this school of thought.

Apartheid: a policy or system of segregation on the grounds of race. *A Disquisition on Government* was written at a time of racial apartheid in the American South.

Aristocratic government: a form of government where nobility holds power. This was Europe's standard system prior to the French Revolution, and it has continued influence today.

Calhoun doctrine: a term coined by historian Robert R. Russell that refers to the principles laid out by John C. Calhoun, which declared that the federal government could not legally abolish slavery in the American South.

Civil Rights Movement: a social movement in the United States that sought to achieve legal equality for African Americans. Ironically, Calhoun's case for minority rights was revived to defend equal civil rights for blacks, despite the fact that he supported slavery.

Classical republicanism: an ideology built on the concepts of mixed government, civic virtue, and liberty. *Disquisition* fits this wider body of political thought.

Concurrent majority: a term coined by Calhoun that refers to the principle that political action requires the unanimous consent of states.

Confederate States of America: the group of seven slave states that split from the United States in 1861. This event led to the American Civil War. Although Calhoun argued for preserving the Union, his ideas later inspired the formation of the Confederate States of America.

Congress: the legislature of the United States that consists of the Senate and the House of Representatives.

Consociational democracy: a democracy based on joint-consensual rule rather than a majority. Calhoun's idea of a concurrent majority inspired this concept, introduced by twentieth-century political scientist Arend Lijphart.

Constitution: a set of political principles used to establish a state. The US Constitution, signed in 1787, replaced the Articles of Confederation with a stronger central government. As an anti-Federalist, Calhoun opposed this.

Constitutional Convention: a meeting held in Philadelphia in 1787 to lay the groundwork for a new constitution. Calhoun felt the US Constitution infringed upon states' rights.

Constitutional government: a government whose authority is defined by a written document. Calhoun argued that this form of government best safeguarded against a "tyranny of the majority."

Declaration of Independence: the document signed in 1776 that formally announced the split of the American colonies from Britain. The American debate over a potential "tyranny of the majority," which is central to *Disquisition*, dates to this period.

Demagogue: a political figure who manipulates the emotions of the masses for his own gain.

Democracy: a form of government where citizens exercise power either directly or through elected representatives who act in their name.

Democratic Party: an American political party that developed in the 1790s from Anti-Federalist factions that favored states' rights.

Despotism: a political system where a single ruler exercises absolute authority over his subjects. Calhoun argued against oppression and despotism.

Early republic: the period between the American Revolution (1776) and the outbreak of the American Civil War (1861). Calhoun wrote *Disquisition* at the end of this period.

English Commonwealth men: a group of British political thinkers who promoted balanced government in the late seventeenth and eighteenth centuries.

Enlightenment: a cultural and intellectual movement that sought to reform society through the use of reason. Enlightenment thought influenced Calhoun's vision of states' rights and slavery.

European Union: an economic and political union of 28 members established in 1993 with the Treaty of Maastricht. It built on the European Economic Community, established by the Treaty of Rome in 1957.

Federalism: a system of government that grants executive power to a central governing authority. In *Disquisition*, Calhoun argued against a strong federal government.

Federalists: politicians who supported the proposed American Constitution between 1787 and 1789, as well as a republic built on strong central government and limited sovereignty for states. Calhoun was an Anti-Federalist: a proponent of states' rights.

Founding Fathers: statesmen and political leaders who sparked the American Revolution and framed the American Constitution. The Founding Fathers supported a strong federal government, but they stressed a separation of powers to prevent any one branch of government from gaining excessive control.

Free Soil Party: an American political party, active between 1848 and 1852, composed of anti-slavery activists. Calhoun opposed this group because he backed continued slavery.

French Revolution: an upheaval in 1790s France that ousted the monarchy and established a republic, the form of government Calhoun argued was the best to prevent a tyranny of the majority.

Hegemony: the dominance of one social group over another. *Disquisition* offered spirited support for the brutal, hegemonic power of slave-holding elites.

Holocaust: the genocide of Jews and others by the Nazis during World War II. Since the Holocaust, Calhoun's defense of pluralist democracy and minority rights has been revived and extended.

House of Representatives: a legislative chamber of the United States Congress; the other is the Senate.

International relations: the study of diplomatic and political relationships among different countries. Some of Calhoun's arguments in *Disquisition* have been applied to international relations.

Italian Renaissance: a period of cultural and intellectual ferment between the thirteenth and sixteenth centuries. During this period, a greater emphasis was placed on balanced government to avoid excesses of power.

Jeffersonian republicanism: a political movement in the early nineteenth century that grew from the ideas of Thomas Jefferson and advocated for states' rights and the interests of farmers.

Legislature: a political assembly with the power to debate, pass, and repeal laws. In 1828, Calhoun drafted "Exposition and Protest" at the request of the South Carolina legislature.

Majority government: a government formed by a political party with an absolute majority. In *Disquisition*, John C. Calhoun advocated the protection of states' rights against such majorities.

Majority rule: governance based on decisions by an elected majority.

Mexican–American War (1846–8): an armed conflict between Mexico and the United States. It stirred tensions between the South and North over whether the new US territories would be free or slave states.

Minority and subject parties: as defined by Calhoun, these groups are not in control of the popularly elected executive and legislative branches of a central government.

Monarchy: a government where a single and usually hereditary figure, such as a king or queen, holds absolute power. Calhoun viewed certain aspects of a constitutional monarchy in a positive light, but he stressed that state rights' must be protected against majority rule.

Nationalism: the ideology that advocates the political independence of a country. Daniel Webster, a critic of Calhoun, was a nationalist who argued that America must have a strong national identity.

Natural rights: rights believed to apply to all human beings. In supporting slavery, Calhoun opposed this doctrine.

Nazi Party: a political party headed by Adolf Hitler that ruled Germany from 1933 to 1945. The Nazis slaughtered more than six million Jews during the Holocaust. Afterwards, Calhoun's *Disquisition* was revived as a defense of minority rights.

Neo-Federalists: A group of nineteenth-century political thinkers who backed the undivided sovereignty of the national government. It included Daniel Webster, who was a staunch critic of Calhoun.

Northern states: non-slave-holding states that did not secede from the United States during the Civil War.

Nullification: the theory that a state has a right to invalidate a federal law that it deems unconstitutional. This was one of Calhoun's key principles in *Disquisition*.

Nullification Crisis: a crisis sparked by South Carolina's threat to invalidate federal tariffs within its territory. John C. Calhoun promoted this doctrine in promoting states' rights.

Numerical majority: a term Calhoun coined to refer to a state dominated by a group elected through majority votes.

Penny press: the steam-powered presses used in the middle of the nineteenth century. This press reduced the cost of newspaper production and made news accessible to middle- and working-class audiences. Calhoun argued that such technology and greater freedom of the press threatened political and social order.

Plantocracy: a ruling class dominated by plantation owners. Calhoun defended the interest of this group.

Pluralism: a political system in which power is distributed among multiple groups. Calhoun advocated this system.

Pluralist democracy: the practice of pluralism in a democratically elected government.

Presbyterianism: a branch of reformed Protestantism that emerged in Britain during the English Civil War. As a young man, Calhoun was taught by a Presbyterian minister in Georgia.

Racial genocide: the systematic murder of racial or ethnic groups. The Nazis carried out racial genocide during World War II. This led to a revival of Calhoun's ideas of democratic pluralism and minority rights.

Republican Party: a political party founded in 1854, mainly composed of anti-slavery activists. Calhoun argued instead for the continued practice of slavery.

Republican Period: a movement that started in the late eighteenth century and favored a national government to counter the influence of political majorities in individual states. By the mid-1800s, Republicans became a leading force in US anti-slavery efforts.

Scotch-Irish: a group of immigrants, largely descended from Scottish and English colonists in Ireland, who played an important role in settling the American frontier in the eighteenth and nineteenth centuries. Calhoun was of Scotch-Irish heritage.

Secession: the political act of withdrawing from a nation. In 1861, seven slave states seceded from the United States to form the Confederate States of America, sparking the American Civil War. Although Calhoun argued for preserving the Union, his ideas later inspired southern secession.

Secretary of war: an office within the United States government responsible for administering the United States Army. Calhoun served in this office from 1817 to 1825.

Senate: a legislative chamber of the United States. The other is the House of Representatives.★

Six Nations Confederacy: a group of six Native American tribes that inhabited the western portion of New York State. In *Disquisition*, Calhoun defends such minority interests.

Social evolutionists: thinkers of the nineteenth century who believed that humankind progressed through stages from primitive to civilized. Calhoun used this theory to justify the enslavement of blacks.

Southern states: states within the American Republic in which the economies were primarily based on slave labor on agricultural plantations. In *Disquisition*, Calhoun defended states' rights, with a stress on southern states in particular.

States' rights: in American politics, this refers to the right of a state to veto or nullify any law passed by the larger central government. Calhoun defended states' rights against a tyranny of the majority.

Supreme Court: the United States federal court that acts as the head interpreter of the constitution and holds ultimate power over all federal and state courts. It considers any attempt by states to nullify its laws as unconstitutional.

Tariff of 1828: a tariff or tax that the US Congress imposed on foreign nations. It aimed to protect industry in the American North, but it had adverse effects on the American South.

Tariffs: taxes imposed on goods destined for export or import. In South Carolina, Calhoun's native state, federal tariffs passed by Congress in the 1820s provoked widespread discontent and threats of secession.

The Kingdom of Poland: a state ruled by an elective monarchy from 1569 until 1795. Poland was ruled by a legislative body in which all members possessed a right to veto proceedings. In *Disquisition*, Calhoun cited this system as one that protected minority rights.

Thirteen Colonies: the territories that declared independence from the British monarchy in 1776. This action first raised the central themes in Calhoun's *Disquisition*, including the proper role of government and the potential of tyranny of the majority.

Tyranny of the majority: the fear that popular democracies can devolve into oppressive political systems or despotic regimes. Calhoun defended states' rights against a tyranny of the majority.

United Nations: an international body founded in 1945 to promote international cooperation among countries. After the United Nations formed, John C. Calhoun's ideas regarding democratic pluralism and minority rights came into use.

United Nations General Assembly: a principal body of the United Nations that gives every member nation equal representation. One mission of the UN is to monitor abuses of power and oppression.

United Nations Security Council: the United Nations branch charged with keeping international peace.

Universal Declaration of Human Rights: a document adopted by the United Nations General Assembly on December 10, 1948. This declaration reflects Calhoun's ideas regarding minority rights.

Universal equality: the belief that there is fundamental equality between human beings. In supporting slavery, Calhoun opposed this doctrine.

US Congress: the legislative body of the federal government. Calhoun defended states' rights against the oppression of the federal government.

Veto: a constitutional right to negate a decision made by a legislative or executive branch of government. Calhoun argued unsuccessfully that states should have veto power over laws passed by the federal government.

Virginia Report: a document drafted in 1800 following the Kentucky and Virginia Resolutions of 1798 and 1799. It took the position that states could invalidate laws enacted by Congress that they deemed unconstitutional. The US Constitution and Supreme Court opposed this.

War of 1812: a war between Britain and the United States fought from 1812 to 1815. Also called the second American war for independence, the War of 1812 took place during Calhoun's political career and reinforced existing political tensions.

World War II (1939–45): a global conflict fought between the Axis Powers (Germany, Italy, and Japan) and the victorious Allied Powers (United Kingdom and its colonies, the former Soviet Union, and the United States).

PEOPLE MENTIONED IN THE TEXT

John Adams (1735–1826) was the second president of the United States. In 1788, he was the first to use the term "tyranny of the majority." This key concept appears in John C. Calhoun's *A Disquisition on Government*.

Aristotle (384–322 B.C.E.) was an ancient Greek philosopher and one of the great philosophers of all time. His ideas regarding human nature and political organization influenced Calhoun's arguments in *Disquisition*.

Irving H. Bartlett (1923–2006) was professor and chair of American civilization at the University of Massachusetts, Boston. He is the author of *John C. Calhoun: A Biography*.

Darryl Baskin: an American political scientist who praised Calhoun's *Disquisition* for its vision of pluralism, meaning that multiple states could share power. Calhoun expresses his pluralistic views through his concept of the   concurrent majority.

Guy Story Brown is professor of philosophy and literature at Lubbock Christian University. He is the author of *Calhoun's Philosophy of Politics*.

H. Lee Cheek Jr. (b. 1960) is dean of social sciences and professor of political science at East Georgia College. This expert on Calhoun argues that *Disquisition* is relevant to contemporary political science.

Noam Chomsky (b. 1928) is an American linguist and political critic. His book *Manufacturing Consent: The Political Economy of the Mass Media* (1988) analyzed how business and government interests use the media to shape public opinion that supports their interests. Calhoun argued that technology and a greater freedom of the press threatened political and social order.

Richard N. Current (1912–2012) was a historian of the American South. He disputed the idea that Calhoun is relevant to contemporary political science.

Henry William de Saussure (1763–1839) was a South Carolina lawyer who founded one of the state's leading Federalist newspapers. He was one of Calhoun's law instructors.

Alexis de Tocqueville (1805–59) was a French political thinker best known for his work *Democracy in America*. He popularized the term "tyranny of the majority."

Peter F. Drucker (1909–2005) was an Austrian-born American economist, political scientist, and philosopher. He has asserted that Calhoun's concept of the concurrent majority remains relevant because it can be analytically separated from his historical defense of slavery.

Ronnie W. Faulkner is associate professor at Campbell University. He has argued with Michael M. Gunter, his co-author of a journal article on Calhoun, that the United Nation's Security Council's veto is "the supreme manifestation of Calhoun's theory of the concurrent majority."

Mitchell Franklin (1902–86) was a professor of law and philosophy at the University of Buffalo. Two years after the formation of the United Nations, Franklin remarked that this organization reflected Calhoun's concept of the concurrent majority.

Lani Guinier (b. 1950) is a professor of law at Harvard University and a civil rights activist. She has argued that an electoral system based on the principle of the concurrent majority would better protect the interests of racial minorities in the United States.

Michael M. Gunter (b. 1943) is professor of political science at Tennessee Technological University. With Ronnie W. Faulkner, his co-author of a journal article on Calhoun, he has argued that the United Nations Security Council's veto is "the supreme manifestation of Calhoun's theory of the concurrent majority."

Alexander Hamilton (1755–1804) was a Founding Father of the United States and an influential politician in the early period of the republic. He argued that the national government needed sufficient power to counter the influence of political majorities in individual states.

Louis Hartz (1919–86) was an American political scientist, best known for his scholarship on the history of the liberal tradition in the United States. He vehemently denied that *Disquisition* contained any principles of enduring worth, urging that the text could not be read outside the author's defense of the institution of slavery.

Adolf Hitler (1889–1945) was the leader of the Nazi Party and dictator of Germany during World War II. Hitler's actions in killing more than six million Jews illustrated the "tyranny of the majority" that Calhoun had warned of in the nineteenth century.

Thomas Hobbes (1588–1679) was an English philosopher best remembered for his book *Leviathan* that established what is now known as social contract theory. Hobbes championed government, specifically the monarchy, as the supreme defense against the chaotic "state of nature." His ideas may have influenced Calhoun regarding human nature and government.

Richard Hofstadter (1916–70) was an American historian and public intellectual. He criticized Calhoun's text as one that defended the minority privileges of slave owners rather than minority rights.

Andrew Jackson (1767–1845) was the seventh president of the United States.

Thomas Jefferson (1743–1826) was the principal author of the Declaration of Independence and the third president of the United States. Thomas Jefferson argued for a separation of powers to prevent government abuse and oppression.

John F. Kennedy (1917–1963) was the 35th president of the United States. He honored John C. Calhoun posthumously as one of the five most important senators in American history.

Ross M. Lence was a professor of political science at the University of Houston from 1971–2006. He is the author of *Union and Liberty*, a book on the political philosophy and writings of John C. Calhoun.

Arend Lijphart (b. 1936) is a political scientist specializing in comparative politics. He introduced a form of democracy based on joint-consensual rule rather than majority power that was inspired by John C. Calhoun's concurrent majority.

Abraham Lincoln (1809–65): the 16th president of the United States, who freed American slaves through the Emancipation Proclamation, which went into effect on January 1, 1863. Calhoun's *Disquisition* defended the rights of slave holders.

Walter Lippmann (1889–1974) was a public intellectual whose book *Public Opinion* is a seminal text in the field of media studies. Calhoun argued that technology and a greater freedom of the press threatened the existing political and social order.

Niccolò Machiavelli (1469–1527) was a Florentine historian and political philosopher. He promoted a "balanced government" to avoid excessive abuses.

James Madison (1751–1836) was a political theorist and the fourth president of the United States. During the framing of the US Constitution, Madison advocated less power for the central government and more for individual states.

John Stuart Mill (1806–73) was a British philosopher and political economist who further popularized the term "tyranny of the majority."

John O'Sullivan (b. 1942) is a British Conservative commentator and former speechwriter and policy writer for British Prime Minister Margaret Thatcher. He criticized Lani Guinier's attempt to revive Calhoun's ideas as destructive to the cohesiveness of American society.

Thomas Paine (1737–1809) was an English pamphleteer and supporter of the American and French Revolutions. He was a proponent of natural rights and universal equality—in contrast to Calhoun, who rejected these principles in supporting slavery.

James H. Read is professor of political science at College of Saint Benedict and Saint John's University. He is the author of *Majority Rule Versus Consensus: The Political Thought of John C. Calhoun*.

Arthur M. Schlesinger Jr. (1917–2007) was a historian of American liberalism. He has asserted the relevance of Calhoun's concurrent majority in modern politics, arguing that it can be separated from his defense of slavery.

Stephen Skowronek (b. 1951) is a political science professor at Yale University. He has remarked that the recent use of Calhoun's ideas by liberal thinkers demonstrates the flexibility of the American political tradition and political ideas in general.

Hermann von Holst (1841–1904) was a German American historian who helped introduce German methods of historical research in American Universities. He has argued that the "largest share of the responsibility for [the Civil War] rests on his [Calhoun's] shoulders."

Hanes Walton Jr. (1941–2013) was a political science professor at the University of Michigan and a prominent scholar of African American political movements. He argued in a 1971 book that African Americans could draw from *Disquisition* in demanding a right to veto public policy laws affecting their interests.

Daniel Webster (1782–1852) was a prominent Massachusetts senator of the pre-Civil War period. He criticized Calhoun in advocating a strong federal government and American national identity.

Clyde Wilson (b. 1941) is emeritus professor of history at the University of South Carolina. He is the author of *The Essential Calhoun*.

WORKS CITED

WORKS CITED

Bartlett, Irving H. *John C. Calhoun: A Biography*. New York and London: W.W. Norton & Company, 1993.

Baskin, Darryl. "The Pluralist Vision of John C. Calhoun." *Polity* 2, no. 1 (1969): 49–65.

Bolt, William K. "Founding Father and Rebellious Son: James Madison, John C. Calhoun and the Use of Precedents." *American Nineteenth-Century History* 5, no. 3 (2004): 15–16.

Brown, Guy Story. *Calhoun's Philosophy of Politics.* Macon, GA: Mercer University Press, 2000.

Calhoun, John C. *A Disquisition on Government.* Edited by H. Lee Cheek Jr. South Bend, IN: St Augustine's Press, 2007.

Speeches of John C. Calhoun and Daniel Webster in the Senate of the United States on the Enforcing Bill. Boston: Beals, Homer & Co., 1833.

Calhoun, John C. and Ross M. Lence (ed.). *Union and Liberty.* Indianapolis: Liberty Fund, 1992.

Calhoun, John Caldwell and H. Lee Cheek Jr. *John C. Calhoun: Selected Writings and Speeches*. Washington DC: Regnery Publishing, 2003.

Calhoun, John Caldwell and Clyde N. Wilson (ed.). *The Essential Calhoun*. New Brunswick: Transaction Publishing, 2000.

Cheek Jr., H. Lee. *Calhoun and Popular Rule: The Political Theory of the Disquisition and Discourse*. Columbia: University of Missouri Press, 2001.

Current, Richard N. *John C. Calhoun*. New York: Washington Square Press, 1963.

"John C. Calhoun, Philosopher of Reaction." *Antioch Review* 3 (1943): 23–34.

Faulkner, Ronnie W., and Michael M. Gunter. "UN Ambassador Daniel Patrick Moynihan and the Calhounian Connection." *Teaching Political Science: Politics in Perspective* 13, no. 2 (1986): 68–81.

Feller, Daniel. "John C. Calhoun." In *Reader's Guide to American History*, edited by Peter J. Parish, 89–90. Chicago: Fitzroy Dearborn Publishers, 1997.

Franklin, Mitchell. "The Roman Origin and the American Justification of the Tribunitial or Veto Power in the Charter of the United Nations." *Tulane Law Review* 22 (October 1947): 24–61.

Hofstadter, Richard. *The American Political Tradition and the Men Who Made It*. New York: A. A. Knopf, 1948.

Kuic, Vukan. "John C. Calhoun's Theory of the Concurrent Majority." *American Bar Association Journal* 69 (1983): 482–88.

Lijphart, Arend. "Majority rule versus democracy in deeply divided societies." *Politikon: South African Journal of Political Studies* 4 (1977): 113–26.

Nevin, John. *John C. Calhoun and the Price of Union*. Baton Rouge: Louisiana State University Press, 1993.

O'Sullivan, John. "Mistaken Identities." *National Review* 48, no. 22 (1996): 50–56.

Read, James Jr., Arthur M. *The Age of Jackson*. Boston: Little, Brown and Company, 1945.

Skowronek, Stephen. "The Reassociation of Ideas and Purposes: Racism, Liberalism and the American Political Tradition." *American Political Science Review* 100, no. 3 (2006): 385–401.

Tocqueville, Alexis de. *Democracy in America*. Translated by Henry Reeve. Vol. 2. New York: Adlard and Saunders, 1838–40.

Von Holst, Herman. *John C. Calhoun*. Boston: Houghton Mifflin Co., 1882.

THE MACAT LIBRARY
BY DISCIPLINE

AFRICANA STUDIES

Chinua Achebe's *An Image of Africa: Racism in Conrad's Heart of Darkness*
W. E. B. Du Bois's *The Souls of Black Folk*
Zora Neale Huston's *Characteristics of Negro Expression*
Martin Luther King Jr's *Why We Can't Wait*
Toni Morrison's *Playing in the Dark: Whiteness in the American Literary Imagination*

ANTHROPOLOGY

Arjun Appadurai's *Modernity at Large: Cultural Dimensions of Globalisation*
Philippe Ariès's *Centuries of Childhood*
Franz Boas's *Race, Language and Culture*
Kim Chan & Renée Mauborgne's *Blue Ocean Strategy*
Jared Diamond's *Guns, Germs & Steel: the Fate of Human Societies*
Jared Diamond's *Collapse: How Societies Choose to Fail or Survive*
E. E. Evans-Pritchard's *Witchcraft, Oracles and Magic Among the Azande*
James Ferguson's *The Anti-Politics Machine*
Clifford Geertz's *The Interpretation of Cultures*
David Graeber's *Debt: the First 5000 Years*
Karen Ho's *Liquidated: An Ethnography of Wall Street*
Geert Hofstede's *Culture's Consequences: Comparing Values, Behaviors, Institutes and Organizations across Nations*
Claude Lévi-Strauss's *Structural Anthropology*
Jay Macleod's *Ain't No Makin' It: Aspirations and Attainment in a Low-Income Neighborhood*
Saba Mahmood's *The Politics of Piety: The Islamic Revival and the Feminist Subject*
Marcel Mauss's *The Gift*

BUSINESS

Jean Lave & Etienne Wenger's *Situated Learning*
Theodore Levitt's *Marketing Myopia*
Burton G. Malkiel's *A Random Walk Down Wall Street*
Douglas McGregor's *The Human Side of Enterprise*
Michael Porter's *Competitive Strategy: Creating and Sustaining Superior Performance*
John Kotter's *Leading Change*
C. K. Prahalad & Gary Hamel's *The Core Competence of the Corporation*

CRIMINOLOGY

Michelle Alexander's *The New Jim Crow: Mass Incarceration in the Age of Colorblindness*
Michael R. Gottfredson & Travis Hirschi's *A General Theory of Crime*
Richard Herrnstein & Charles A. Murray's *The Bell Curve: Intelligence and Class Structure in American Life*
Elizabeth Loftus's *Eyewitness Testimony*
Jay Macleod's *Ain't No Makin' It: Aspirations and Attainment in a Low-Income Neighborhood*
Philip Zimbardo's *The Lucifer Effect*

ECONOMICS

Janet Abu-Lughod's *Before European Hegemony*
Ha-Joon Chang's *Kicking Away the Ladder*
David Brion Davis's *The Problem of Slavery in the Age of Revolution*
Milton Friedman's *The Role of Monetary Policy*
Milton Friedman's *Capitalism and Freedom*
David Graeber's *Debt: the First 5000 Years*
Friedrich Hayek's *The Road to Serfdom*
Karen Ho's *Liquidated: An Ethnography of Wall Street*

John Maynard Keynes's *The General Theory of Employment, Interest and Money*
Charles P. Kindleberger's *Manias, Panics and Crashes*
Robert Lucas's *Why Doesn't Capital Flow from Rich to Poor Countries?*
Burton G. Malkiel's *A Random Walk Down Wall Street*
Thomas Robert Malthus's *An Essay on the Principle of Population*
Karl Marx's *Capital*
Thomas Piketty's *Capital in the Twenty-First Century*
Amartya Sen's *Development as Freedom*
Adam Smith's *The Wealth of Nations*
Nassim Nicholas Taleb's *The Black Swan: The Impact of the Highly Improbable*
Amos Tversky's & Daniel Kahneman's *Judgment under Uncertainty: Heuristics and Biases*
Mahbub Ul Haq's *Reflections on Human Development*
Max Weber's *The Protestant Ethic and the Spirit of Capitalism*

FEMINISM AND GENDER STUDIES

Judith Butler's *Gender Trouble*
Simone De Beauvoir's *The Second Sex*
Michel Foucault's *History of Sexuality*
Betty Friedan's *The Feminine Mystique*
Saba Mahmood's *The Politics of Piety: The Islamic Revival and the Feminist Subject*
Joan Wallach Scott's *Gender and the Politics of History*
Mary Wollstonecraft's *A Vindication of the Rights of Women*
Virginia Woolf's *A Room of One's Own*

GEOGRAPHY

The Brundtland Report's *Our Common Future*
Rachel Carson's *Silent Spring*
Charles Darwin's *On the Origin of Species*
James Ferguson's *The Anti-Politics Machine*
Jane Jacobs's *The Death and Life of Great American Cities*
James Lovelock's *Gaia: A New Look at Life on Earth*
Amartya Sen's *Development as Freedom*
Mathis Wackernagel & William Rees's *Our Ecological Footprint*

HISTORY

Janet Abu-Lughod's *Before European Hegemony*
Benedict Anderson's *Imagined Communities*
Bernard Bailyn's *The Ideological Origins of the American Revolution*
Hanna Batatu's *The Old Social Classes And The Revolutionary Movements Of Iraq*
Christopher Browning's *Ordinary Men: Reserve Police Batallion 101 and the Final Solution in Poland*
Edmund Burke's *Reflections on the Revolution in France*
William Cronon's *Nature's Metropolis: Chicago And The Great West*
Alfred W. Crosby's *The Columbian Exchange*
Hamid Dabashi's *Iran: A People Interrupted*
David Brion Davis's *The Problem of Slavery in the Age of Revolution*
Nathalie Zemon Davis's *The Return of Martin Guerre*
Jared Diamond's *Guns, Germs & Steel: the Fate of Human Societies*
Frank Dikotter's *Mao's Great Famine*
John W Dower's *War Without Mercy: Race And Power In The Pacific War*
W. E. B. Du Bois's *The Souls of Black Folk*
Richard J. Evans's *In Defence of History*
Lucien Febvre's *The Problem of Unbelief in the 16th Century*
Sheila Fitzpatrick's *Everyday Stalinism*

Eric Foner's *Reconstruction: America's Unfinished Revolution, 1863-1877*
Michel Foucault's *Discipline and Punish*
Michel Foucault's *History of Sexuality*
Francis Fukuyama's *The End of History and the Last Man*
John Lewis Gaddis's *We Now Know: Rethinking Cold War History*
Ernest Gellner's *Nations and Nationalism*
Eugene Genovese's *Roll, Jordan, Roll: The World the Slaves Made*
Carlo Ginzburg's *The Night Battles*
Daniel Goldhagen's *Hitler's Willing Executioners*
Jack Goldstone's *Revolution and Rebellion in the Early Modern World*
Antonio Gramsci's *The Prison Notebooks*
Alexander Hamilton, John Jay & James Madison's *The Federalist Papers*
Christopher Hill's *The World Turned Upside Down*
Carole Hillenbrand's *The Crusades: Islamic Perspectives*
Thomas Hobbes's *Leviathan*
Eric Hobsbawm's *The Age Of Revolution*
John A. Hobson's *Imperialism: A Study*
Albert Hourani's *History of the Arab Peoples*
Samuel P. Huntington's *The Clash of Civilizations and the Remaking of World Order*
C. L. R. James's *The Black Jacobins*
Tony Judt's *Postwar: A History of Europe Since 1945*
Ernst Kantorowicz's *The King's Two Bodies: A Study in Medieval Political Theology*
Paul Kennedy's *The Rise and Fall of the Great Powers*
Ian Kershaw's *The "Hitler Myth": Image and Reality in the Third Reich*
John Maynard Keynes's *The General Theory of Employment, Interest and Money*
Charles P. Kindleberger's *Manias, Panics and Crashes*
Martin Luther King Jr's *Why We Can't Wait*
Henry Kissinger's *World Order: Reflections on the Character of Nations and the Course of History*
Thomas Kuhn's *The Structure of Scientific Revolutions*
Georges Lefebvre's *The Coming of the French Revolution*
John Locke's *Two Treatises of Government*
Niccolò Machiavelli's *The Prince*
Thomas Robert Malthus's *An Essay on the Principle of Population*
Mahmood Mamdani's *Citizen and Subject: Contemporary Africa And The Legacy Of Late Colonialism*
Karl Marx's *Capital*
Stanley Milgram's *Obedience to Authority*
John Stuart Mill's *On Liberty*
Thomas Paine's *Common Sense*
Thomas Paine's *Rights of Man*
Geoffrey Parker's *Global Crisis: War, Climate Change and Catastrophe in the Seventeenth Century*
Jonathan Riley-Smith's *The First Crusade and the Idea of Crusading*
Jean-Jacques Rousseau's *The Social Contract*
Joan Wallach Scott's *Gender and the Politics of History*
Theda Skocpol's *States and Social Revolutions*
Adam Smith's *The Wealth of Nations*
Timothy Snyder's *Bloodlands: Europe Between Hitler and Stalin*
Sun Tzu's *The Art of War*
Keith Thomas's *Religion and the Decline of Magic*
Thucydides's *The History of the Peloponnesian War*
Frederick Jackson Turner's *The Significance of the Frontier in American History*
Odd Arne Westad's *The Global Cold War: Third World Interventions And The Making Of Our Times*

LITERATURE

Chinua Achebe's *An Image of Africa: Racism in Conrad's Heart of Darkness*
Roland Barthes's *Mythologies*
Homi K. Bhabha's *The Location of Culture*
Judith Butler's *Gender Trouble*
Simone De Beauvoir's *The Second Sex*
Ferdinand De Saussure's *Course in General Linguistics*
T. S. Eliot's *The Sacred Wood: Essays on Poetry and Criticism*
Zora Neale Huston's *Characteristics of Negro Expression*
Toni Morrison's *Playing in the Dark: Whiteness in the American Literary Imagination*
Edward Said's *Orientalism*
Gayatri Chakravorty Spivak's *Can the Subaltern Speak?*
Mary Wollstonecraft's *A Vindication of the Rights of Women*
Virginia Woolf's *A Room of One's Own*

PHILOSOPHY

Elizabeth Anscombe's *Modern Moral Philosophy*
Hannah Arendt's *The Human Condition*
Aristotle's *Metaphysics*
Aristotle's *Nicomachean Ethics*
Edmund Gettier's *Is Justified True Belief Knowledge?*
Georg Wilhelm Friedrich Hegel's *Phenomenology of Spirit*
David Hume's *Dialogues Concerning Natural Religion*
David Hume's *The Enquiry for Human Understanding*
Immanuel Kant's *Religion within the Boundaries of Mere Reason*
Immanuel Kant's *Critique of Pure Reason*
Søren Kierkegaard's *The Sickness Unto Death*
Søren Kierkegaard's *Fear and Trembling*
C. S. Lewis's *The Abolition of Man*
Alasdair MacIntyre's *After Virtue*
Marcus Aurelius's *Meditations*
Friedrich Nietzsche's *On the Genealogy of Morality*
Friedrich Nietzsche's *Beyond Good and Evil*
Plato's *Republic*
Plato's *Symposium*
Jean-Jacques Rousseau's *The Social Contract*
Gilbert Ryle's *The Concept of Mind*
Baruch Spinoza's *Ethics*
Sun Tzu's *The Art of War*
Ludwig Wittgenstein's *Philosophical Investigations*

POLITICS

Benedict Anderson's *Imagined Communities*
Aristotle's *Politics*
Bernard Bailyn's *The Ideological Origins of the American Revolution*
Edmund Burke's *Reflections on the Revolution in France*
John C. Calhoun's *A Disquisition on Government*
Ha-Joon Chang's *Kicking Away the Ladder*
Hamid Dabashi's *Iran: A People Interrupted*
Hamid Dabashi's *Theology of Discontent: The Ideological Foundation of the Islamic Revolution in Iran*
Robert Dahl's *Democracy and its Critics*
Robert Dahl's *Who Governs?*
David Brion Davis's *The Problem of Slavery in the Age of Revolution*

Alexis De Tocqueville's *Democracy in America*
James Ferguson's *The Anti-Politics Machine*
Frank Dikotter's *Mao's Great Famine*
Sheila Fitzpatrick's *Everyday Stalinism*
Eric Foner's *Reconstruction: America's Unfinished Revolution, 1863-1877*
Milton Friedman's *Capitalism and Freedom*
Francis Fukuyama's *The End of History and the Last Man*
John Lewis Gaddis's *We Now Know: Rethinking Cold War History*
Ernest Gellner's *Nations and Nationalism*
David Graeber's *Debt: the First 5000 Years*
Antonio Gramsci's *The Prison Notebooks*
Alexander Hamilton, John Jay & James Madison's *The Federalist Papers*
Friedrich Hayek's *The Road to Serfdom*
Christopher Hill's *The World Turned Upside Down*
Thomas Hobbes's *Leviathan*
John A. Hobson's *Imperialism: A Study*
Samuel P. Huntington's *The Clash of Civilizations and the Remaking of World Order*
Tony Judt's *Postwar: A History of Europe Since 1945*
David C. Kang's *China Rising: Peace, Power and Order in East Asia*
Paul Kennedy's *The Rise and Fall of Great Powers*
Robert Keohane's *After Hegemony*
Martin Luther King Jr.'s *Why We Can't Wait*
Henry Kissinger's *World Order: Reflections on the Character of Nations and the Course of History*
John Locke's *Two Treatises of Government*
Niccolò Machiavelli's *The Prince*
Thomas Robert Malthus's *An Essay on the Principle of Population*
Mahmood Mamdani's *Citizen and Subject: Contemporary Africa And The Legacy Of Late Colonialism*
Karl Marx's *Capital*
John Stuart Mill's *On Liberty*
John Stuart Mill's *Utilitarianism*
Hans Morgenthau's *Politics Among Nations*
Thomas Paine's *Common Sense*
Thomas Paine's *Rights of Man*
Thomas Piketty's *Capital in the Twenty-First Century*
Robert D. Putman's *Bowling Alone*
John Rawls's *Theory of Justice*
Jean-Jacques Rousseau's *The Social Contract*
Theda Skocpol's *States and Social Revolutions*
Adam Smith's *The Wealth of Nations*
Sun Tzu's *The Art of War*
Henry David Thoreau's *Civil Disobedience*
Thucydides's *The History of the Peloponnesian War*
Kenneth Waltz's *Theory of International Politics*
Max Weber's *Politics as a Vocation*
Odd Arne Westad's *The Global Cold War: Third World Interventions And The Making Of Our Times*

POSTCOLONIAL STUDIES

Roland Barthes's *Mythologies*
Frantz Fanon's *Black Skin, White Masks*
Homi K. Bhabha's *The Location of Culture*
Gustavo Gutiérrez's *A Theology of Liberation*
Edward Said's *Orientalism*
Gayatri Chakravorty Spivak's *Can the Subaltern Speak?*

PSYCHOLOGY

Gordon Allport's *The Nature of Prejudice*
Alan Baddeley & Graham Hitch's *Aggression: A Social Learning Analysis*
Albert Bandura's *Aggression: A Social Learning Analysis*
Leon Festinger's *A Theory of Cognitive Dissonance*
Sigmund Freud's *The Interpretation of Dreams*
Betty Friedan's *The Feminine Mystique*
Michael R. Gottfredson & Travis Hirschi's *A General Theory of Crime*
Eric Hoffer's *The True Believer: Thoughts on the Nature of Mass Movements*
William James's *Principles of Psychology*
Elizabeth Loftus's *Eyewitness Testimony*
A. H. Maslow's *A Theory of Human Motivation*
Stanley Milgram's *Obedience to Authority*
Steven Pinker's *The Better Angels of Our Nature*
Oliver Sacks's *The Man Who Mistook His Wife For a Hat*
Richard Thaler & Cass Sunstein's *Nudge: Improving Decisions About Health, Wealth and Happiness*
Amos Tversky's *Judgment under Uncertainty: Heuristics and Biases*
Philip Zimbardo's *The Lucifer Effect*

SCIENCE

Rachel Carson's *Silent Spring*
William Cronon's *Nature's Metropolis: Chicago And The Great West*
Alfred W. Crosby's *The Columbian Exchange*
Charles Darwin's *On the Origin of Species*
Richard Dawkin's *The Selfish Gene*
Thomas Kuhn's *The Structure of Scientific Revolutions*
Geoffrey Parker's *Global Crisis: War, Climate Change and Catastrophe in the Seventeenth Century*
Mathis Wackernagel & William Rees's *Our Ecological Footprint*

SOCIOLOGY

Michelle Alexander's *The New Jim Crow: Mass Incarceration in the Age of Colorblindness*
Gordon Allport's *The Nature of Prejudice*
Albert Bandura's *Aggression: A Social Learning Analysis*
Hanna Batatu's *The Old Social Classes And The Revolutionary Movements Of Iraq*
Ha-Joon Chang's *Kicking Away the Ladder*
W. E. B. Du Bois's *The Souls of Black Folk*
Émile Durkheim's *On Suicide*
Frantz Fanon's *Black Skin, White Masks*
Frantz Fanon's *The Wretched of the Earth*
Eric Foner's *Reconstruction: America's Unfinished Revolution, 1863-1877*
Eugene Genovese's *Roll, Jordan, Roll: The World the Slaves Made*
Jack Goldstone's *Revolution and Rebellion in the Early Modern World*
Antonio Gramsci's *The Prison Notebooks*
Richard Herrnstein & Charles A Murray's *The Bell Curve: Intelligence and Class Structure in American Life*
Eric Hoffer's *The True Believer: Thoughts on the Nature of Mass Movements*
Jane Jacobs's *The Death and Life of Great American Cities*
Robert Lucas's *Why Doesn't Capital Flow from Rich to Poor Countries?*
Jay Macleod's *Ain't No Makin' It: Aspirations and Attainment in a Low Income Neighborhood*
Elaine May's *Homeward Bound: American Families in the Cold War Era*
Douglas McGregor's *The Human Side of Enterprise*
C. Wright Mills's *The Sociological Imagination*